home cooking with jean-georges

home cooking with

ALSO BY JEAN-GEORGES VONGERICHTEN

Asian Flavors WITH GENEVIEVE KO

Simple to Spectacular WITH MARK BITTMAN

Jean-Georges: Cooking at Home with a Four-Star Chef WITH MARK BITTMAN

jean-georges

my favorite simple recipes

jean-georges vongerichten

WITH GENEVIEVE KO

Clarkson Potter/Publishers
New York

Published in the United States by Clarkson Potter/Publishers,
an imprint of the Crown Publishing Group,
a division of Random House, Inc., New York.
www.crownpublishing.com
www.clarksonpotter.com

CLARKSON POTTER is a trademark and POTTER with
colophon is a registered trademark of Random House, Inc.

Library of Congress Cataloging-in-Publication Data
Vongerichten, Jean-Georges.
    Home cooking with Jean-Georges / Jean-Georges
Vongerichten, Genevieve Ko. — 1st ed.
        p.   cm.
    Includes bibliographical references and index.
    1. Cooking.   2. Cookbooks.   I. Ko, Genevieve.   II. Title.
TX714.V658 2011
641.5—dc22   2010053808

ISBN 978-0-307-71795-5
eISBN 978-0-307-95328-5

Printed in China

Book design by Stephanie Huntwork
Jacket design by Stephanie Huntwork
Jacket photography by John Kernick

10   9   8   7   6   5   4   3   2   1

First Edition

contents

welcome

On my first drive up to Waccabuc, a rural town in upstate New York, I told my wife, Marja, that I probably wouldn't like the place. We had decided to buy a weekend home to spend unhurried time with our young daughter, Chloe; my older children, Cedric and Louise; and our extended family. I had assumed we would find a house in the Hamptons. I love the beach and looked forward to cooking the fresh seafood caught off the coast.

But as we wound through the grassy hills some fifty miles north of Manhattan, I began warming to the idea of being secluded. We pulled up a gravel drive and caught sight of two neat, white Cape Cod houses. As we walked through the airy main house, looking out the double-height windows at the lake below and the woods beyond, we realized we had found the perfect home away from home.

The walls of windows resembled our fishbowl city apartment in a modern glass tower, but here, the only gawkers were wide-eyed deer. From room to room, the color scheme of soft whites and elephant grays closely matched those of my flagship restaurant, where I spend more time than anywhere else. A fireplace at one end of the expansive kitchen reminded me of my childhood

home in Alsace, as did the outside root cellar built of large, old stones. And the grassy hill that stretched down and out to the lake and woods beyond was like a deep exhalation. After more than thirty-five years of working nonstop to build a restaurant empire, I could finally let go and relax.

I started cooking the day we moved in. I found it incredibly relaxing. Almost immediately, I was struck by how long it had been since I had cooked at home. I grew up cooking at home with my mother and grandmother, but basically stopped when I left to apprentice. It felt so great to finally cook in my own home kitchen. I had really missed it—the simple acts of preparing a meal and then sitting down with my family to enjoy it.

. . .

I was born and raised in Alsace, France, in a small village not far from the gothic spires of the Strasbourg cathedral and its surrounding cobblestone streets and storybook shops. Nestled in the countryside, our family home was flanked by a river on one side and verdant fields on the other. In the distance, vineyards produced wines as white and crisp as snowy Alsatian mornings. Our nearest neighbors were more than a mile away, and we lived close enough to the steep slopes of the Vosges to ski every day in winter. Outside the kitchen door, our family kept a vast garden. Beyond that lay the woods, which served as a playground for me and my two younger brothers in the summer. My brothers and I lived with our older sister, our parents, and grandparents in the same home our great-grandfather had built in 1833.

I woke up to the smells of choucroute—onions, cabbage, pork—and at the end of the day, my mom and grandma baked the most amazing tarts—the whole house smelled like butter and sugar. Even before I could reach the countertops, I eagerly helped my mom and grandma in the kitchen. They taught me the fundamentals of rustic country cooking and our family's culinary secrets, like how a splash of dark coffee cuts through the richness of goose stew, and how lightly crushed anise seeds release their fragrance into crumbly cookies.

It wasn't long before I had mastered the family repertoire—and begun improving upon it. Even though I was only in grade school, I knew when to add a little more salt to the mustard vinaigrette, a little more pepper to the schnitzel. When I walked through our herb garden, I became inspired by its scents; I started tossing a little dill and parsley into the warm potato salad and creating bouquets garnis for braises. My family nicknamed me "Palate" and my mom and grandma regularly called on me to taste and adjust the seasonings of their dishes.

I was expected to take over the family coal business. My parents enrolled me in an engineering program; I hated it enough to get myself kicked out. The kitchen was my refuge.

To celebrate my sixteenth birthday, my parents took me to L'Auberge de l'Ill, a Michelin three-star restaurant near our home. That meal changed my life. I had prepared foie gras terrines in my home but had never tasted foie gras wrapped around a whole Perigord truffle and baked in hand-rolled puff pastry. Nor had I tried *saumon soufflé* or *mousseline de grenouilles*. Each dish thrilled me and renewed the passion for food that I had first discovered at my mom's side.

My mom convinced chef Paul Haeberlin to take me on as an apprentice. On my first day at work, I was assigned the most tedious task in the entire kitchen: preparing pheasants. Anyone who has ever plucked a bird, still warm from the hunt, knows just how hard it is to pull the feathers cleanly from the skin. And I wasn't allowed to wet the birds first, which causes the feathers to release more easily, because Chef Haeberlin wanted the skins dry to enhance their texture and flavor. To remove any remaining bits of fuzz, I had to carefully singe the skin to keep it whole and further dry it. After a long day of inhaling the pheasants' pungent scent, I stood knee-deep in

feathers, reeking of game. That was when I knew I wanted to be a chef. I was assigned the worst task in the kitchen and yet I wanted to perfect it, to pluck faster and more cleanly, and eventually, to turn that pheasant into a beautiful dish.

The next day, I peeled what seemed like a ton of potatoes, carefully removing only the paper-thin skins to leave smooth rounds. My passion for perfection and a newfound desire to become a great chef kept me happy on my feet for sixteen hours straight. Whatever I had to give up—parties with friends, afternoons skiing, a comfortable life—was worth the sacrifice of pursuing my dream. That evening, I told my parents that I wouldn't be returning home to the family business after my apprenticeship. My father didn't speak to me for a year.

I learned to take the same beautiful ingredients we had at home—pike and carp from the Rhine, wild game from the woods—and treat them as a chef would. When I made tarte tatin with my mom, we threw butter, sugar, and apples in the pan and baked them with puff pastry on top. During my apprenticeship, I had to create a caramel with the sugar and butter, then layer paper-thin slices of apples in perfect circles in the hot caramel. And the pastry had to go on at just the right time or the dessert was considered ruined.

After completing my apprenticeship and my military service, I went south to work for star chef Louis Outhier at the restaurant L'Oasis, housed in a French Riviera villa in La Napoule, a small village near Cannes. Surrounded by an abundance of fresh, leafy herbs and olive oil, I developed an affinity for light, clean flavors. I moved on to Lyon to work under master chef Paul Bocuse. Living along the banks of the Saône, near the Pont de Collonges, I learned Bocuse's traditional yet innovative style of French cuisine. I turned Lyonnaise fish quenelles and drew out the natural succulence of Bresse chickens. I thought I had a solid grasp of cooking at this point. And then I received a call with a new challenge.

Outhier had landed a lucrative deal with the Mandarin Oriental hotel chain and been named the chef of all of its restaurants. He asked me to head the kitchen of the renowned Oriental in Bangkok. So, in November 1980, I arrived on the other side of the world. As I wound past the Chao Phraya River on the drive from the airport, I was overwhelmed by the heady scents drifting in the window. I asked the taxi driver to pull over. I hopped out, picked up the first dish I saw on that street corner, and started slurping. It was a bowl of tom yum gai—and it changed my life. There were so many flavors I had never tasted before: coconut, galangal, lemongrass, lime leaves, lime juice, cilantro, shiitakes . . . It was the most incredible, intense soup. I loved it so much, I had it for dinner every night after work.

During the day, I created classic French dishes; at night, I trolled the city, tasting all the local cuisine I could. On my one day off, I visited the huge open-air markets, fingering and smelling herbs and spices I'd never seen before. Having fallen in love with Thai flavors, I developed a similar passion for other Asian cuisines when I left Bangkok to head Outhier's kitchens in Singapore, Hong Kong, and Osaka.

Outhier then sent me to Boston and, in 1986, on to New York City to be the chef de cuisine of the Lafayette. I knew the stakes were high; I was scared. I'm a country boy, and this was New York. I worked seventeen- and eighteen-hour days—Outhier's style of French cooking is very involved—and I never left the restaurant. When I finally ventured out a year later, I visited Chinatown, where I experienced a déjà vu that took me back to Thailand's markets. Thrilled to find galangal and lemongrass, I began to subtly incorporate Southeast Asian ingredients into my dishes. I slowly shifted my menu away from rich French classics when I noticed diners asking for the creamy sauces on the side and then leaving them untouched. I began making my sauces with fruit juices and oils, infusing them with different aromatics, creating intensely flavorful and nuanced dishes with a distinctive clean quality.

When I opened my first restaurant, JoJo, I called my brother Philippe to come and help me.

Together, we built a warm, timeless space that evoked the comforts of our childhood home. The menu of the cozy, bistro-like restaurant fused the rustic home cooking of my youth with innovative techniques and Asian ingredients. Though they showcased groundbreaking flavors, all of the dishes were simple and deeply comforting. To convince Philippe to stay in town, I trained him to manage the front of the house. It wasn't hard—we share an intuitive understanding of good service. The graciousness we learned from our mom and grandma translated into impeccable dining room service that made even the most jaded New Yorkers feel at home. In the midst of a deepening recession in 1990, JoJo opened to rave reviews and established a lengthy roster of regulars.

We then opened Vong and, later, my flagship restaurant, Jean Georges. More than any other place, the restaurant Jean Georges became my home. I prepared dishes that reflected my background: decidedly French young garlic soup with crisp frog legs, elegant turbot in Chateau Chalon sauce, foie gras with a restrained richness, and Asian influences in everything from marinated hamachi to broiled five-spice squab. My staff became family, and not just because Philippe served as general manager. I went on to open more than two dozen restaurants across the globe with my team. And I continued to work eighteen-hour days, six days a week.

. . .

On my fiftieth birthday, I decided to give myself a gift that most people take for granted: two-day weekends. Since I was sixteen, I had only taken Sundays off; that's just enough time to sleep in a little and run a few errands. Now, for the first time in my adult life, I get to relax. Even though my country home is just an hour or so drive from Manhattan, it's completely secluded, with no cell phone towers for miles. I can't get a signal up there, and I don't plan to try. Instead, I play with Chloe and my new grandson, Olivier, catch up with Cedric and Louise, and spend time with Marja. And I cook. For the first time in thirty-five years, I am cooking at home. My mind is spinning with ideas.

The dishes I cook in the country are decidedly simple and unfussy—even boneless chicken breasts!—and yet they are some of my favorites. As soon as I clear the breakfast dishes, I think about what to have for lunch. Usually, it's a delicious salad composed of whatever I happen to find at the farmer's market. In the spring, I pile radishes on butter lettuce and in the summer, I toss tomatoes and wax beans with a goat cheese dressing.

While I love nothing more than a simple lunch, dinner is another affair. Although I don't do anything too elaborate, I do like to prepare full meals, including dessert, especially for company.

Growing up, I ate dinner with my extended family every night. With a dozen or more gathered around our big farmhouse table, we passed dishes of our native French-German specialties and swapped stories about the day. We shared the leisurely meal as a family, just as we had prepared it as a family.

My father and one of my grandmothers always cooked an appetizer or two. My mom, an excellent cook, handled the main course, while my other grandmother—the best baker I know—always made dessert. My siblings and I gathered ingredients; I appointed myself the task of tasting everything. Our family life revolved around the kitchen.

Nearly fifty years later, it still does. As at my childhood home in Alsace, everyone gravitates toward the kitchen in our country home. And that's how I like it. There's a warmth there, a casual intimacy in preparing a meal as a family. My wife cooks her specialties and, along with my sister-in-law, fixes snacks for all the kids. My brother helps me prep vegetables and builds fires for grilling. My son, Cedric, handles the meat and fish, while my older daughter, Louise, makes great cocktails. (Of course, I haven't given up my job as taster-in-chief.)

We sit down to large platters of food meant to be shared, like the ones I grew up with. My home-cooked meals are a far cry from the

formality of my plated restaurant dishes, but they deliver the same intricate balance of flavors and textures that make them delicious. As a rule, I start with the best ingredients, then combine them in easy, surprising ways. Tiny lavender buds lighten my take on veal scaloppine, and serranos add a kick to sea bass with potatoes. I gravitate toward simple, honest dishes, like sweet pea soup and bittersweet chocolate chantilly.

My goal is to spend as much time as possible with my family while cooking and eating good food. I want everyone to feel at ease and welcome in my home. My weekends behind the stove at home restore me and deliver a pleasure that's impossible to find any other way. While my weekends are meant to be my time away from work—and they are—they also now inspire my work. I can't wait to share my family's meals and all that I've learned while preparing them. Relaxing with my family is just about the best thing that's happened to my cooking in a long time. I hope you'll feel the same way cooking from this book.

cocktails and appetizers

WHEN THE COOKING STARTS IN MY house, my family and guests usually stop what they're doing and head toward the kitchen. Knowing that everyone will gather around the kitchen counter, I set out appetizers for them to have a little snack. As at my restaurants, I pack my starters with flavor because they're little dishes: the smaller the bite, the more intense the flavor needs to be. My popcorn and pecans get hits of spice, which I like to buy from Le Sanctuaire. At home, I keep my food casual, making family-style platters of my take on finger foods. When guests dip their own crudités in my super-savory anchovy sauce and slather spicy crab on toasts, they start to have fun.

Or maybe it's the cocktails that get the party going. My daughter Louise handles the bar, just as she did when she was the beverage director of my restaurant Mercer Kitchen in New York City. She always chooses just the right aperitif. I create my cocktails the way I create my dishes: by balancing bright acidity with a little heat, a little sweetness. As always, I use high-quality ingredients and splurge on good liquor. The cocktails I like the most have intense, clean flavors, like my gingery margarita. Here are a few of our family favorites, including the homemade soda and lemonade we make for the kids.

Once guests start eating and drinking, I can finish up at the stove. I love sharing my kitchen with others, and this way I can have a little company while I pull together dinner.

THE BEAUTY of the Manhattan is its smooth simplicity. That's why it's so important to use the best ingredients available. For the vermouth, I prefer Antica Formula Carpano, which has a fresh and complex herbaceousness. Near my country house is the Tuthilltown Spirits whiskey distillery, and their New York Whiskey tastes great in this drink. To embellish on the original, I add just a touch of brandied sour cherries and their juices. You can buy them at a specialty foods store.

brandied cherry
manhattan MAKES 1 DRINK

¼ cup whiskey

2 tablespoons vermouth

1½ teaspoons brandied sour cherry juice

3 brandied sour cherries, skewered on a cocktail pick

Fill a cocktail shaker with ice. Add the whiskey, vermouth, and cherry juice. Stir well. Strain into a martini glass and garnish with the cherries.

THIS IS EASILY my favorite party drink. I combine the white wine of my native Alsace with the tropical fruit flavors I first came to love when I cooked in Thailand. It's a natural pairing and tastes amazing with just about anything. Best of all, it's meant to be made ahead of time, leaving me free to finish up dinner prep.

passion fruit sangria   MAKES 6 TO 8 DRINKS

1 bottle (750 ml) dry
   Gewürztraminer
¾ cup orange liqueur,
   preferably Gran Gala
6 tablespoons Simple Syrup
   (recipe follows)
7 tablespoons passion fruit
   puree (see Pantry, page 253)
1 cup fresh orange juice
1 orange, quartered and thinly
   sliced
1 lime, quartered and thinly
   sliced
1 cup blackberries, halved
¼ pineapple, peeled, cored, and
   cut into 1-inch batons
15 thin slices peeled fresh
   ginger

In a pitcher or punch bowl, combine the Gewürztraminer, orange liqueur, simple syrup, passion fruit puree, orange juice, orange, lime, blackberries, pineapple, and ginger and stir well. Refrigerate for 2 hours before serving.

When ready to serve, fill wine glasses with ice. Divide the sangria, with the fruit, among the glasses.

simple syrup   MAKES 6 TABLESPOONS

6 tablespoons sugar

Bring the sugar and 6 tablespoons water to a boil in a small saucepan, stirring to dissolve the sugar. Remove from the heat and cool to room temperature.

IF WE HAD a family drink, this would be it. (Underage kids excepted, of course.) It's my older daughter Louise's favorite, and she makes this margarita perfectly for all of us on the weekends. I love the heat of the ginger balanced by aged tequila. Be sure to use high-quality aged tequila here. Otherwise, the drink will taste like spring break gone wild.

ginger margarita   MAKES 1 DRINK

1 lemon wedge

Kosher salt

1½ tablespoons Ginger Syrup (page 244)

1 tablespoon orange liqueur, preferably Cointreau

3 tablespoons golden tequila, preferably Sauza Tres Generaciones Añejo

Run the lemon wedge over the rim of a lowball glass and then dip the rim into salt. Reserve the lemon wedge.

Fill a cocktail shaker with ice. Add the ginger syrup, orange liqueur, and tequila. Cover and shake like crazy for about 10 seconds. If you think you've shaken it enough, shake some more.

Strain into the glass, then add ice. Squeeze the reserved lemon wedge over and drop into the glass. Serve immediately.

TO GET THROUGH the winter months, I rely on bright, in-season citrus like blood oranges. A nice, dry bubbly heightens their vibrant sweetness, as does orange-flavored liqueur. For the flavors to bind properly, you need to combine—but not stir—the ingredients before pouring into flutes. If you can't find Crémant d'Alsace, my sparkling wine of choice, a dry cava will work as well.

blood orange bellini   MAKES 8 DRINKS

1¼ cups fresh blood orange
 juice
1 bottle (750 ml) dry Crémant
 d'Alsace, chilled
3 tablespoons orange liqueur,
 preferably Cointreau

Pour the juice, Crémant, and orange liqueur into a large glass pitcher. Immediately and carefully pour into 8 champagne flutes and serve.

THIS IS IDEAL as a summer refresher, but tastes great any time of year. I love combining lemon and thyme in savory dishes, and they taste great together in this sweet drink, too. Lemon thyme, which has a light citrus note, is available in specialty stores and is easy to grow in your garden. I prefer using brands of citrus vodka that have clean flavors, like Skyy and Grey Goose Le Citron. Other times, I leave the vodka out altogether—definitely when I'm serving this to kids!

lemon-thyme vodka lemonade MAKES 1 DRINK

3 lemon wedges
Sugar
¼ cup Lemon-Thyme Syrup
   (recipe follows)
¼ cup citrus vodka
¼ cup club soda
1 sprig fresh thyme, preferably
   lemon thyme

Run 1 lemon wedge over the rim of a highball glass; dip the rim into sugar. Reserve the lemon wedge.

Put the remaining 2 lemon wedges in a cocktail shaker along with the syrup and vodka. Muddle hard, breaking the lemon skins to release their oils. Cover and shake.

Carefully fill the rimmed glass with ice. Pour the syrup mixture into the glass, lemon wedges and all. Top off with the club soda, then squeeze the reserved lemon wedge over before dropping it into the glass. Garnish with the thyme sprig and serve immediately.

lemon-thyme syrup MAKES 1 CUP

¾ cup sugar
1 small bunch fresh thyme, preferably
   lemon thyme (½ ounce)

In a small saucepan, heat 1 cup water and the sugar to boiling, stirring to dissolve the sugar. Add the thyme, remove from the heat, and let stand until cool. Strain through a fine-mesh sieve, pressing to extract as much liquid as possible. Cover and refrigerate for up to 3 days.

EVEN THOUGH I originally conceived of this as my take on homemade ginger ale, I'm hesitant to call it that. It's such a far cry from the sugary bottled stuff. It has an intense gingery heat that's heightened by the acidity from the lemon. Be sure to use a fresh bottle of club soda here. (I prefer the little bottles of Schweppes.) You need the fizziness to deliver the flavor.

ginger lemon soda   MAKES 1 DRINK

¼ cup Ginger Syrup (page 244)
¾ cup club soda

Fill a highball glass with ice. Pour in the syrup, then the soda. Stir with a straw and serve immediately.

THIS SIMPLE starter always brings me back to Provence, where I trained as a young chef. There, we served this sea-salty dip with scallions and red bell peppers, but now fennel is my favorite. This dip is so good, it works with any combination of vegetables; pick from my suggestions below. And if you think you don't like anchovies, you have to try this. The milk mellows the intensity of the fish and the garlic and makes the dip incredibly creamy.

crudités with anchovy dip   SERVES 8 TO 12

ANCHOVY DIP

1 garlic clove, peeled
4 salted anchovy fillets packed in oil, rinsed and patted dry
⅓ cup whole milk
1 tablespoon plus 1 teaspoon champagne vinegar
1 teaspoon kosher salt
3½ tablespoons extra-virgin olive oil

CRUDITÉS

Red or yellow Belgian endive, quartered lengthwise
Celery, tough strings removed, cut into sticks
Fennel bulbs, cut into wedges
Small, thin carrots, peeled
Breakfast and globe radishes
Sugar snap peas, halved lengthwise
Summer squash, cut into spears
Red, yellow, or orange bell peppers, cut into sticks

Put the garlic in a small saucepan and cover with cold water. Bring to a boil, then drain. Repeat once, then put in a bowl of cold water. When cool, drain again.

Puree the garlic in a blender with the anchovies, milk, vinegar, and salt until smooth. With the machine running, add the oil in a steady stream. Continue blending until smooth and creamy.

Transfer to a serving bowl and serve with crudités.

c'est bon When serving raw bell peppers, I like to use a vegetable peeler to remove the paper-thin skin. You can get rid of their slight bitterness that way.

THERE ARE few snacks I enjoy more than popcorn. Maybe it's because I like watching movies to relax on the weekends. But also, there's something about its light crispness that's so appealing—it goes well with just about any cocktail. When I don't have fresh rosemary on hand—or when I'm craving a little heat—I toss popcorn with a pinch of piment d'Espelette, smoked paprika, or Korean chile powder.

rosemary popcorn   MAKES 12 CUPS

½ cup popcorn kernels

2 teaspoons extra-virgin olive oil, plus more as needed

1 tablespoon fresh rosemary leaves, finely chopped

1 teaspoon kosher salt

Pop the popcorn kernels in a popper or on your stovetop according to the package directions. Transfer to a very large bowl. Drizzle with the oil, then sprinkle with the rosemary and salt. Toss until the kernels are evenly seasoned. Serve immediately.

THESE NUTS smell wonderful while baking. I use them in Grilled Chicken Salad with Apples and Roquefort (page 130), but I also eat them as a snack all the time. When I have some left, I put out a bowl for guests. They keep well for up to three days, but they rarely last that long in my house.

candied paprika pecans MAKES 2½ CUPS

2½ cups pecan halves

¼ cup light corn syrup

1 teaspoon smoked or regular coarse sea salt or kosher salt

½ teaspoon smoked hot paprika

½ teaspoon ground allspice

Preheat the oven to 350°F. Line a rimmed baking sheet with parchment paper or a Silpat.

Toss the pecans with the corn syrup, salt, paprika, and allspice in a large bowl until evenly coated. Spread in a single layer on the prepared pan. Bake, rotating the pan once, until the pecans are deep golden brown and fragrant, about 10 minutes.

Immediately transfer to a large bowl and toss continuously until the nuts separate into individual pieces. If necessary, separate clumps with your fingers. Let cool completely. Store in an airtight container.

AS MUCH AS I love to eat crunchy snacks, I also really enjoy the juicy savory bite of olives. But I temper their saltiness with the anise aroma of fennel, the sweetness of orange, and a little heat. Over the years, we've been able to get an increasing variety of olives—even in our local markets. I like combining different Mediterranean varieties and always buy them unpitted.

orange and fennel marinated olives   MAKES 1½ CUPS

1 cup large green brine-cured olives, preferably Sevillano and Castelvetrano

½ cup kalamata olives

½ teaspoon fennel seeds

⅛ teaspoon crushed red chile flakes

2 (4-inch) strips fresh orange zest (removed with a vegetable peeler)

1 cup extra-virgin olive oil

If you're able to find Sevillano olives, rinse them under cold water for 5 minutes, then soak them in cold water for 2 hours. Drain well.

Combine the olives in a medium bowl.

Toast the fennel seeds in a small skillet over medium heat until fragrant, about 1 minute. Add the chile flakes and toast until just fragrant, about 30 seconds. Remove from the heat and add the orange zest and oil. Steep until cool.

Pour the oil mixture over the olives. Cover and marinate at room temperature for 6 hours or refrigerate for up to 3 days.

artichokes vinaigrette SERVES 4

4 large globe artichokes (12 to
  14 ounces each)
¼ cup kosher salt, plus more
  to taste
2 medium shallots, finely
  chopped
¼ cup sherry vinegar
¼ cup extra-virgin olive oil
Freshly ground black pepper

To snap the stem off an artichoke, put it on the counter on its side, with the globe on your left side and the stem on your right. Hold down the globe firmly with your left hand and place your right palm at the base of the artichoke, where the globe meets the stem. The side of your right thumb should be pressed against the bottom of the globe. In one swift, firm motion, press down the stem. The whole stem, including the tiny fibers that connect it to the base, should snap off. Repeat with the remaining artichokes.

Put the artichokes in a wide pot and cover with water. Add ¼ cup salt, cover the pot, and bring to a boil over high heat. Reduce the heat to medium, uncover, and simmer until the artichokes are very tender and a knife pierces through them easily, about 1 hour. Using a slotted spoon, very carefully transfer to a colander and let cool to warm, about 10 minutes.

Meanwhile, whisk together the shallots, vinegar, oil, and a pinch each of salt and pepper.

Arrange the artichokes, pointed sides up, on a serving plate. Gently press down on the tops so they open like blooming flowers. Drizzle half of the vinaigrette all over the artichokes. Pour the remaining vinaigrette into a serving bowl for dipping.

Instruct your guests to pluck the leaves from the artichokes, dip them in the vinaigrette, and eat by scraping the flesh from the base of the leaves with their
teeth. When all the leaves are eaten, cut the hearts in
half, scoop out and discard the chokes, and divide the
hearts among the diners.

MAKE THIS quintessential summer dish when ripe, fresh tomatoes and fragrant basil are abundant at farm stands (or in your garden). Seek out an artisan sourdough to complement them. Be sure to assemble these as soon as the toast is ready. The hot bread releases the juices and tangy sweetness of the tomatoes.

heirloom tomato crostini   SERVES 4

4 ripe heirloom tomatoes
4 large slices good sourdough
    bread
Extra-virgin olive oil
Kosher salt and freshly ground
    black pepper
8 fresh basil leaves

Cut the tomatoes in half from top to bottom, remove the cores, then cut crosswise into ¼-inch-thick slices.

Set an oven rack 4 inches from the broiler heat source. Preheat the broiler.

Arrange the bread in a single layer on a broiler pan. Generously drizzle oil on both sides of the bread. Broil, turning once, until golden, about 2 minutes.

Immediately arrange the tomato slices, overlapping slightly, on the toast. Season with salt and pepper and tear the basil leaves over the top. Drizzle with a little more oil and serve immediately.

c'est bon If my broiler is in use, I use my toaster oven instead. There are few things I like more than grilled bread, but it would be too overpowering here. You definitely want the subtlety of toasted bread.

MY GRANDMOTHER used to take whatever extra livers we had—calf, chicken, goose—and cook them with bacon and a splash of Cognac. She chopped the mixture with a mezzaluna, creating a rustic spread. I swap pancetta for the bacon and puree the mixture in a food processor to create a creamy mousse.

chicken liver and pancetta crostini   SERVES 8

1¾ ounces sliced pancetta (about 3 slices), finely diced

¼ cup finely diced yellow onion

8 ounces chicken livers, deveined

Kosher salt and freshly ground black pepper

2 tablespoons unsalted butter

2 tablespoons Cognac

Extra-virgin olive oil

4 large slices good sourdough bread

1 garlic clove, halved

4 fresh sage leaves, thinly sliced

Preheat the grill or broiler to medium-high.

Cook the pancetta in a medium skillet over medium-high heat until the fat renders, about 1 minute. Add the onion and cook, stirring frequently, until dark golden brown, about 6 minutes. Transfer to the bowl of a food processor.

Generously season the livers with salt and pepper. Add the butter to the skillet you used to cook the pancetta and onion and melt over high heat. Add the livers in a single layer and cook, turning once, until browned on the outside and rosy pink in the center, about 4 minutes. Be careful—the livers pop and sputter when cooking. Do not overcook them. Immediately transfer to the food processor with the butter in the pan.

Add the Cognac to the skillet, tilt the pan toward the flame, and flambé. Let boil until reduced by half. Transfer to the food processor and pulse the mixture until smooth. Taste and adjust the seasonings.

Generously drizzle oil on both sides of the bread. Grill, turning once, until grill marks appear, about 3 minutes. Rub the hot toast with the garlic. Divide the liver mousse among the toast slices and spread evenly. Drizzle with a little more oil and sprinkle with the sage. Cut each toast into quarters and serve immediately.

c'est bon Overcooked livers have an unpleasant, metallic taste. You can take them out of the pan and cut into them while they're cooking to see if they're done. And because they're not uniform in size, be sure to remove the smaller ones first.

AT MY RESTAURANTS, we make our own yogurt, carefully culturing milk at 93°F for hours. At home, I pop open a container of good whole-milk yogurt from the store. Just be sure to stir that creamy top layer into the rest of the yogurt before using it. The richness and tanginess pair perfectly with sweet beets. While I prefer boiled beets in this dish, roasted beets work well, too.

beets with yogurt and chervil SERVES 4

Kosher salt and freshly ground
  black pepper
1 pound beets, preferably a
  mix of red, candy-striped,
  and gold, trimmed and
  scrubbed
1 cup plain whole-milk yogurt
1 tablespoon plus 1 teaspoon
  balsamic vinegar
3 tablespoons fresh chervil,
  coarsely chopped
Baby beet greens, optional
1 tablespoon extra-virgin
  olive oil

Bring a large saucepan of water to a boil. Generously salt the water and add the beets. When the water returns to a boil, reduce the heat to medium and simmer until a knife easily pierces through the beets, about 1 hour. Drain. When cool enough to handle, peel and cut into wedges or cubes.

Spoon the yogurt into a serving dish. Scatter the beets on top and drizzle the vinegar over them. Season with salt and pepper and top with the chervil and greens, if using. Drizzle the oil all over.

I LIKE TO serve this family-style: Guests spoon the crab onto the toasts just before eating, so the bread stays crisp. At once creamy and spicy, this starter tastes best with an aperitif like champagne, rosé champagne, or a Grüner Veltliner.

crab toasts with sriracha mayonnaise SERVES 4

4 slices good sourdough bread

3 tablespoons Sriracha Mayonnaise (page 246)

8 ounces picked lump crabmeat, preferably peekytoe, picked over for bits of shell

Crushed red chile flakes, optional

1 lemon, cut into wedges

Toast the bread until golden brown. Cut each slice into 2-inch pieces.

Gently fold the mayonnaise into the crabmeat until well mixed. Spoon the crab mixture into a serving bowl and set inside a larger serving bowl filled with ice to keep cold if desired. Garnish with chile flakes if desired. Serve with the lemon wedges and toasts.

c'est bon My dear friend and seafood supplier Ingrid Bengis gets me the best crab from Maine. It's delicate, sweet, and unbelievably fresh. Find the freshest crab available in a local seafood shop or in your market's refrigerated fish counter; this dish doesn't work with shelf-stable canned crabmeat.

I LOVE TO present this in martini glasses like an old-school shrimp cocktail. The sauce has the horseradish bite of the classic, but with a juicy, sweet freshness from the peach. Traditionally, the shrimp would be chilled first, but I serve them warm for a hit of hot and cold at the same time in each bite.

shrimp with peach cocktail sauce SERVES 4

PEACH COCKTAIL SAUCE

1 large very ripe peach, peeled and pitted
1 tablespoon finely grated peeled fresh horseradish
2 tablespoons grade A maple syrup
1 tablespoon champagne vinegar
1 teaspoon fresh lime juice
1 teaspoon sugar
½ teaspoon kosher salt

SHRIMP

¼ cup champagne vinegar
5 sprigs fresh thyme
1 dried bay leaf, plus fresh leaves for garnish
1 tablespoon plus 1 teaspoon kosher salt
1 pound large (16- to 20-count) shrimp, shelled and deveined, tails kept intact
Celery leaves, for garnish

To make the sauce, grate the peach on the large holes of a box grater over a bowl to collect all the pulp and juices. Add the horseradish, maple syrup, vinegar, lime juice, sugar, and salt. Stir until well combined. Cover and refrigerate until cold.

Meanwhile, cook the shrimp: Combine 1 quart water, the vinegar, thyme, dried bay leaf, and salt in a large saucepan. Bring to a boil over high heat, then adjust the heat to maintain a bare simmer. Add the shrimp and poach until just opaque throughout, about 3 minutes. Drain and discard the thyme and bay leaf.

Fill martini glasses or a shallow bowl with the sauce. Hang the shrimp around the edge of the glasses or bowl and garnish with celery leaves and fresh bay leaves. Serve immediately.

c'est bon The best way to peel a peach is to choose one that's ripe enough for the skin to slip off naturally. Otherwise, cut a slit in one end of a peach and plunge it into boiling water. Take it out as soon as the peel begins to curl back from the slit, about 10 seconds. When cool enough to handle, remove the peel.

salads

WHEN I WAS A CHILD, VEGETABLES made up most of the spread on the table, which always included a big salad. To "shop" for her salad ingredients, my mom didn't have to go far. We kept a lot of herbs in our garden, and our neighbors grew a variety of vegetables. She never traveled more than a few miles to get all the produce she wanted. And despite living in New York, neither do I. Every Saturday morning, my young daughter, Chloe, and I stop by the Union Square Greenmarket before we drive up to the country. We visit our favorite farmers and ask them for the best they've got. Once we're in the country, we make another stop at Table Local Market. This charming store carries only produce from nearby farms and strongly supports sustainable agriculture, which I strongly believe in.

Salads are built on contrast—crunchy, tender, chewy, creamy, snappy, crisp. I often keep my greens, other vegetables, and dressings separate until close to the end, adjusting the seasonings of each component to best enhance its natural flavors. I then compose them, layering or tossing depending on the ingredients. That isn't to say these are fussy salads—they're not. It's just that they were created to make the most of the vegetables in season. Most of these are best as side salads, but I like them all so much, I often enjoy them as meals in and of themselves, especially when I'm craving a light dinner.

MY GO-TO salad for the fall, this simple combination tastes great with just about everything. Fresh, toasted poppy seeds release a delicious, complex nuttiness into the dressing. You can also add avocado and shrimp or chicken to turn this salad into a complete meal.

mixed greens with yogurt–poppy seed dressing SERVES 8

½ cup plain whole-milk yogurt

2 tablespoons fresh lemon juice

1 tablespoon plus 1 teaspoon honey

1 tablespoon Dijon mustard

1 teaspoon kosher salt

¼ teaspoon freshly ground black pepper

1½ teaspoons poppy seeds

1 pound mixed greens (11 cups)

Whisk together the yogurt, lemon juice, honey, mustard, salt, and pepper until smooth.

Put the poppy seeds in a small skillet and set over medium heat. Cook, shaking the pan occasionally, until the seeds are fragrant and begin to pop, about 3 minutes. Immediately stir into the dressing.

Put the greens in a large bowl, drizzle with the dressing, and gently toss until the leaves are coated. Serve immediately.

WHEN I COMPOSE a salad, I like to pair buttery flavors with bright ones. Here, creamy avocado is offset by the mustard vinaigrette and peppery radishes. I especially like making this in early spring, when the first radishes appear at the market.

butter lettuce, radish, and avocado salad with mustard dressing SERVES 4

1 tablespoon red wine vinegar
2½ teaspoons Dijon mustard
Kosher salt and freshly ground
   black pepper
2 tablespoons grapeseed or
   other neutral oil
2 teaspoons extra-virgin
   olive oil
1 head butter lettuce, torn
8 slender pink French breakfast
   radishes or baby round red
   radishes, halved
1 scallion, white and pale
   green parts only, thinly
   sliced at an angle
2 tablespoons roughly chopped
   fresh dill
1 avocado, halved, pitted,
   peeled, and sliced

Whisk together the vinegar and mustard with a pinch each of salt and pepper. Continue whisking and add the oils in a slow, steady stream until the mixture is emulsified.

Toss the dressing with the lettuce, radishes, scallion, and dill. Top with the avocado and serve.

TANGY GOAT CHEESE makes a perfect salad dressing for wax beans (haricots verts work well here, too). To balance the creamy cheese, I toss the sweet tomatoes with a bright, acidic vinaigrette. Together, they make an amazing summer salad.

wax bean and cherry tomato salad with goat cheese dressing SERVES 4

12 ounces yellow cherry or
  pear tomatoes, halved
1 small shallot, very thinly
  sliced
Kosher salt and freshly ground
  black pepper
1 fresh Thai chile, minced
⅓ cup red wine vinegar
¼ cup plus 1 tablespoon
  extra-virgin olive oil
12 ounces wax beans, trimmed
6 ounces fresh goat cheese,
  softened
2 tablespoons fresh lime juice
12 fresh basil leaves

Season the tomatoes and shallot with salt, then toss with the chile, vinegar, and ¼ cup of the olive oil. Let stand for at least 15 minutes or up to 1 hour.

Meanwhile, bring a large pot of water to a boil. Fill a large bowl with ice and water. Generously season the boiling water with salt and then add the beans. Cook until crisp-tender, about 5 minutes. Drain, transfer to the ice water, and drain again when the beans are room temperature. Cut the beans into 2-inch lengths at an angle.

Combine the goat cheese, lime juice, remaining 1 table-spoon olive oil, and ½ teaspoon salt in a blender. Puree until smooth and fluffy. Toss with the beans until well coated.

Place the wax beans in serving dishes. Top with the tomato mixture. Grind a little black pepper over the whole salad, then tear the basil leaves over the top. Serve immediately.

I'M ALWAYS looking for inspiration when I shop at farmer's markets. The heirloom varieties of summer squash, like Goldbar, Paddle, and 8-Ball, are among my new favorites. To highlight their subtle flavor, I splash them with a simple lemon dressing, then surround them with sharp cheese and peppery greens.

lemony shaved summer squash and pecorino on arugula   SERVES 4

2 large lemons

2 teaspoons kosher salt

Scant ½ cup extra-virgin olive oil

3 ounces arugula, preferably wild or baby (2 cups packed)

2 small or 1 medium yellow squash, sliced paper-thin

2 small or 1 medium zucchini, sliced paper-thin

2 ounces aged pecorino cheese

Freshly ground black pepper

Grate the zest of one of the lemons directly into a jar or bowl with a tight-fitting lid. Squeeze a scant ½ cup juice from the lemons and add to the zest. Add the salt and oil, cover tightly, and shake vigorously.

Spread the arugula in a single layer in a serving dish. Scatter the squash and zucchini on top. Using a vegetable peeler, shave the cheese all over. Shake the dressing again and pour over the salad. Grind the pepper over everything and serve immediately.

c'est bon The best, and really only, way to get perfect paper-thin slices of squash (and any number of other vegetables) is with a mandoline. The traditional, albeit pricey, French mandolines work beautifully, as do the more compact and inexpensive Japanese ones.

THIS IS something I grew up with, a dish my grandmother and mom always served family-style. For me, this combination—a fluffy, snowy mountain of shaved Gruyère with sliced sweet-tart tomato—is home. In Alsace, we sometimes mixed wine vinegar with honey and spices for the dressing, but sherry vinegar has a similar nuanced sweetness that works very well here.

gruyère and tomato salad   SERVES 4

5½ ounces Gruyère cheese

1 large ripe tomato

1 white new (spring) onion or
   2 medium shallots, finely
   chopped

¼ cup thinly sliced fresh
   flat-leaf parsley leaves

Kosher salt and freshly ground
   black pepper

2 tablespoons grapeseed or
   other neutral oil

2 tablespoons sherry vinegar

Grate the Gruyère on the large holes of a box grater directly over a large serving plate. Cut the tomato in half from top to bottom, remove the core, then cut crosswise into ½-inch-thick slices. Arrange the tomato half-moons in a circle around the mound of cheese.

Sprinkle the onion and parsley all over the cheese, then season everything with a pinch of salt and generous grindings of black pepper. Drizzle the oil, then the vinegar, all over the salad and serve immediately.

WHEN I LIVED near Nice in the sunny south of France, I discovered that everyone there has a version of this summer salad. By tasting ones made by everyone from legendary chefs to humble housewives, I came up with my own. My sun-dried tomato vinaigrette makes this version distinctive. The perfumed sweetness of elderflower cordial highlights the concentrated sweetness of the tomatoes. Be sure to use the best sushi-grade bluefin or yellowfin tuna you can find.

niçoise salad with sun-dried tomato vinaigrette SERVES 4

4 large eggs

1 ounce dry-packed sun-dried tomatoes, finely chopped (½ cup)

1 teaspoon grated fresh lemon zest

3 tablespoons elderflower cordial (see Pantry, page 252) or Simple Syrup (page 20)

3 tablespoons extra-virgin olive oil, plus more for cooking

2½ tablespoons fresh lemon juice

2 tablespoons champagne vinegar

Kosher salt and freshly ground black pepper

4 ounces fingerling potatoes

2 ounces haricots verts

1 pound tuna steak, 1¼ inches thick

8 ounces mixed greens (about 5½ cups)

2 ounces black olives, preferably Gaeta, pitted and quartered (⅓ cup)

4 ounces cherry tomatoes, quartered

Bring a small saucepan of water to a boil. Add the eggs and cook for 6 minutes. Drain and run under cold water until cool enough to handle. Peel and cut each in half.

Put the sun-dried tomatoes in a bowl and pour ½ cup hot water over them. Let stand for 15 minutes. Drain well and return to the bowl. Stir in the lemon zest, elderflower cordial, oil, lemon juice, and vinegar. Season to taste with salt and let stand.

Put the potatoes in a medium pot and add enough water to cover by 2 inches. Bring to a boil, season with salt, then reduce the heat to maintain a steady simmer. Cook until a knife pierces through the potatoes easily, about 20 minutes. Drain well. When cool enough to handle, peel and cut into ¼-inch-thick rounds.

Bring a medium pot of water to a boil and generously season with salt. Fill a large bowl with ice and water. Add the haricots verts to the boiling water and cook until crisp-tender, about 5 minutes. Use a slotted spoon to transfer to the ice water bath. Once cool, drain well.

Cut the tuna into 4 even strips. Heat a large skillet over high heat. When hot, add just enough oil to film the bottom. Season the tuna with salt and pepper on all sides, then add to the hot oil. Cook until seared on all sides, about 1 minute per side. The center should be rare. Cut each piece crosswise into ½-inch-thick slices.

Combine the greens, potatoes, beans, olives, tomatoes, and almost all of the dressing in a large bowl. Gently toss until everything is evenly coated. Transfer to a serving platter and top with the tuna and eggs. Drizzle with the remaining dressing.

WHEN WATERMELON ripens in the summer, I treat it simply to make it shine. Blue cheese turns it into a savory, refreshing salad and black pepper ties the whole thing together. To best match the juicy, crisp sweetness of the melon, I look for strong and sharp creamy cheeses. This tastes even better when the watermelon is cold and the cheese is room temperature and soft. In that case, it's easiest to use a spoon to flick nuggets of cheese directly onto the melon.

watermelon and blue cheese salad SERVES 4

½ small watermelon, rind and
    seeds removed, cut into
    1- to 2-inch chunks
2 ounces blue cheese, such as
    Cabrales or Maytag
Extra-virgin olive oil
Maldon salt or other flaky
    sea salt
Freshly ground black pepper

Arrange the watermelon in a layer on a serving platter. Crumble the blue cheese over the melon, then drizzle oil liberally over everything. Season with salt and pepper and serve immediately.

I CRAVE Greek salad year round, so in the winter, when tomatoes don't taste great raw, I make it with roasted beets instead. This began as a home lunch, but I decided to try it out at some of my restaurants, too, and it's turned out to be one of our most popular salads.

greek salad with roasted beets, olives, and feta SERVES 4

4 medium beets, preferably a mix of red, candy-striped, and gold, trimmed and scrubbed

4 tablespoons extra-virgin olive oil

Kosher salt and freshly ground black pepper

6 tablespoons red wine vinegar

¼ cup minced red onion

1 teaspoon minced fresh red Thai chile or crushed red chile flakes, or to taste

2 romaine hearts, halved lengthwise and sliced ½ inch thick at an angle

6 celery heart stalks, sliced ¼ inch thick at an angle, plus celery leaves for garnish

½ cup crumbled feta cheese

3 ounces Niçoise olives, pitted and halved (½ cup)

1 tablespoon fresh oregano leaves, thinly sliced

Preheat the oven to 325°F.

Put the beets on a large sheet of foil. Drizzle with 1 tablespoon of the oil and then season with salt and pepper. Wrap tightly and roast in the oven until a knife pierces through the beets easily, about 1 hour and 15 minutes. Unwrap, and when cool enough to handle, peel the beets and cut into wedges.

Whisk together the vinegar, remaining 3 tablespoons oil, the onion, chile, and 1½ teaspoons salt.

Arrange the beets on 4 serving plates. Drizzle with a little of the dressing and season with salt and pepper. Top with the romaine, celery, feta, and olives. Drizzle the remaining dressing all over. Season with salt and pepper and the oregano. Garnish with celery leaves. Serve immediately.

THIS IS EASILY one of my favorite fall salads. The creaminess of avocado and sour cream is amazing with the spiced zing of the carrots and the toasted, nutty seeds.

carrot and avocado salad with crunchy seeds   SERVES 4

1 tablespoon sunflower seeds

1 tablespoon pumpkin seeds

1 tablespoon white sesame seeds

Cumin and Citrus Roasted Carrots (page 188)

1 avocado, halved, pitted, peeled, and cut into thin wedges

4 cups sprouts, preferably a mix of radish and beet

1 tablespoon plus 1 teaspoon sour cream

Edible flowers, for garnish, optional

Preheat the oven to 350°F.

Spread the sunflower, pumpkin, and sesame seeds in a single layer on a rimmed baking sheet. Bake, stirring occasionally, until lightly toasted and golden, but not golden brown, about 7 minutes. Cool completely.

Arrange the carrots on a serving platter, reserving the accompanying sauce. Put the avocado and then the sprouts on top. Drizzle with the reserved sauce.

Dollop the sour cream over the top, then sprinkle with the seeds. Garnish with flowers if desired. Serve immediately.

endive and sugar snaps with parmesan dressing   SERVES 4

¼ cup freshly grated Parmigiano-Reggiano cheese

2 tablespoons champagne vinegar

1 tablespoon fresh lime juice

¾ teaspoon Dijon mustard

1½ teaspoons kosher salt

½ teaspoon coarsely ground black pepper

3 tablespoons grapeseed or other neutral oil

1½ tablespoons extra-virgin olive oil

8 ounces sugar snap peas, trimmed and strings removed

4 yellow or red Belgian endive, leaves separated

½ cup chopped fresh herb leaves, preferably a mix of flat-leaf parsley, tarragon, dill, and chervil

Combine the cheese, vinegar, lime juice, mustard, salt, and pepper in a blender. Puree until smooth. With the machine running, add the oils through the feed tube in a slow, steady stream to emulsify the mixture.

Bring a pot of water to a boil. Fill a large bowl with ice and water. Generously salt the boiling water and then add the snap peas. Cook just until bright green, about 30 seconds. Drain, transfer to the ice water, and drain again. Slice very thinly at an angle.

Toss the endive and snap peas with the dressing. Top with the herbs.

THIS IS THE type of salad my mom used to make—unfussy and delicious. It's best with fresh spring potatoes and onions, but it hits the spot any time of year. While I love drinking dry white Alsatian whites, I enjoy making this salad with a good Sancerre.

warm alsatian potato salad   SERVES 6

8 large Yukon Gold potatoes
  (2½ pounds), scrubbed
Kosher salt and freshly ground
  black pepper
¼ cup red wine vinegar
¼ cup dry white wine
¼ cup extra-virgin olive oil
⅓ cup thinly sliced fresh
  flat-leaf parsley leaves
¼ cup diced white new
  (spring) onions or shallots

Put the potatoes in a pot, add enough water to cover by 4 inches, and salt generously. Cover partially and bring to a boil over medium-high heat. Boil, stirring occasionally, until the potatoes are very soft and a knife pierces through very easily, about 45 minutes. Drain in a colander and let stand until just cool enough to handle.

Peel and roughly chop the potatoes. Arrange in a single layer in a 3-quart serving dish. Season with salt and pepper and drizzle with the vinegar, wine, and oil. Stir gently until the potatoes soak up the sauce. Top with the parsley and onion, taste and adjust the seasonings, and serve.

lunch

DURING MY CHILDHOOD IN ALSACE, breakfast was big, lunch was huge, and dinner was small. My mom started cooking lunch first thing in the morning: lots of vegetables, rich stews, hefty roasts. By the time dinner rolled around, all we wanted was salad and cheese. Most days, I don't have the time to cook the lunches my mom did, but I do fill my midday meals with a few favorites.

Nowadays, I think of lunch as a casual affair. Sometimes, it's as simple as soup. It won't weigh me down, but it'll still be immensely satisfying. Otherwise, I prefer heartier fare that gives me the energy I need for the rest of the day. Even on weekends, I'm busy shoveling snow in the winter or keeping my beehives in the spring. Sandwiches are more often than not my meal of choice. I compose them carefully, never letting the bread overwhelm the fillings. And I always make my own mayonnaise, which is incredibly easy—by hand, food processor, or blender—and a great way to create a creamy, complex spread.

When I'm feeling ambitious on an otherwise lazy Sunday, I like to create pizzas. (I have to confess that I've been fantasizing about building a pizza oven in my backyard.) Finally, I know that most people don't associate me with pasta, but I've become an aficionado in recent years—Chloe just loves fresh noodles, which are fun to make at home but also can be found in many stores these days. I always finish them in the sauce so that the flavors really cling to the chewy pasta.

quinoa with spinach, goat cheese, and sautéed shiitakes SERVES 4

1 cup quinoa

Kosher salt and freshly ground
  black pepper

6 tablespoons extra-virgin
  olive oil

8 ounces fresh shiitake
  mushrooms, trimmed and
  quartered

6 ounces baby spinach

1 tablespoon plus 1 teaspoon
  red wine vinegar

4 ounces fresh goat cheese,
  crumbled

Toast the quinoa in a large saucepan over medium heat, stirring frequently, until golden brown, about 5 minutes. Stir in 1½ cups water and a pinch of salt and bring to a boil. Cover, reduce the heat to low, and simmer until the water is absorbed, about 15 minutes.

Meanwhile, heat 4 tablespoons of the oil in a large skillet over medium heat. Add the mushrooms and a pinch of salt and pepper and cook, stirring occasionally, until golden brown and tender, about 8 minutes.

Spoon the warm quinoa and mushrooms over the spinach on a serving platter, then drizzle with the vinegar and remaining 2 tablespoons oil. Season with salt and pepper and top with the goat cheese.

FOR YEARS, I've made smooth pureed pea soups; they're always a hit at my restaurants. Recently, I was inspired by my mom to try something new. While visiting New York with my dad, she made a chunky pea and carrot stew with slab bacon and cabbage. I decided to go vegetarian here—doing away with even the chicken stock and creating a tea-like herb infusion instead—and to puree only part of the ingredients, making a light pureed soup with whole peas and sliced carrots scattered throughout. The result is a bowl of spring.

pea potage with carrots, chiles, and mint SERVES 8

3 tablespoons extra-virgin
  olive oil
¾ cup ¼-inch-thick carrot
  rounds
½ medium yellow onion,
  finely diced
1 garlic clove, minced
Kosher salt and freshly ground
  black pepper
5 sprigs fresh mint, plus thinly
  sliced leaves for garnish

2 sprigs fresh rosemary
1 small bunch fresh thyme
  (½ ounce)
5½ cups shelled fresh green
  peas (from 5½ to 6 pounds
  in the pod)
1 fresh green Thai chile,
  minced, or to taste
Sourdough Croutons (recipe
  follows)

c'est bon When fresh peas are not in season (honestly, about eleven months of the year), you can use 5½ cups thawed frozen peas instead. Omit the blanching step and proceed as above, cooking the whole peas just until heated through, about 1 minute.

Heat the oil in a large saucepan over medium heat. Add the carrots, onion, garlic, and a pinch of salt. Cook, stirring frequently, until the vegetables are just tender but not browned, about 15 minutes.

Add 4 cups water and bring to a boil. Remove from the heat. Crush the mint, rosemary, and thyme in your hands and wrap tightly in cheesecloth. Submerge in the water, cover the saucepan, and let steep for 1 hour.

Meanwhile, bring a large pot of water to a boil. Fill a large bowl with ice and water. Add the peas to the boiling water and cook until tender, about 5 minutes. Drain, reserving a bit of the cooking water, and immediately transfer to the ice water. When cool, drain again well, at least 10 minutes.

Put half of the peas in a food processor or blender. Puree until extremely smooth, adding a little liquid from the saucepan if needed and scraping down the sides and bottom of the bowl frequently.

Remove and discard the sachet of herbs from the saucepan. Bring the mixture to a gentle simmer and add the remaining whole peas. Cook just until the peas are heated through, about 5 minutes. Stir in the pea puree and return to a simmer. Season the soup with salt and pepper.

Ladle into serving bowls. Top with the chile, sliced mint, and croutons.

sourdough croutons
MAKES ABOUT 3 CUPS

At home, I like making rustic croutons by tearing bread into bite-size pieces. I want ragged edges— they taste great when cooked and crisped. Croutons are best fresh and take only minutes to make.

1 small loaf good sourdough bread,
   crusts removed, torn into
   ½- to 1-inch pieces
Extra-virgin olive oil

If broiling, arrange the broiler rack 4 inches from the heat source and preheat the broiler. Put the bread in a single layer on a rimmed baking sheet and drizzle generously with oil. Broil until golden brown and crisp, about 2 minutes. Begin checking at 1 minute and stir or turn to brown evenly. If sautéing, heat a large skillet over medium-high heat. Coat the bottom of the skillet with oil and add the bread. Cook, tossing occasionally, until golden brown and crisp, about 5 minutes. Drain on paper towels.

IT'S THE SURPRISING combination of sweet, tart, creamy, and crunchy additions that makes me crave this summery soup. This gazpacho is all about the garnishes.

tomato gazpacho with mozzarella, raspberries, and almonds   SERVES 4

GAZPACHO

4 large ripe beefsteak tomatoes, cored and cut in half through their equators
1 small shallot, coarsely chopped
1 garlic clove, coarsely chopped
½ cup chopped celery heart
½ cup chopped European cucumber
½ cup chopped red bell pepper
½ fresh long red (finger) chile, seeded and chopped
2 teaspoons red wine vinegar
2 teaspoons kosher salt
¼ teaspoon sugar

GARNISHES

8 blanched whole almonds
Extra-virgin olive oil
¾ cup grated fresh mozzarella
8 cherry tomatoes, preferably a mix of colors, sliced ¼ inch thick
1 avocado, halved, pitted, peeled, and cut into ¼-inch cubes
4 raspberries, halved
4 fresh basil leaves, torn
8 very thin slices long red (finger) chile
Fleur de sel or other coarse sea salt
Freshly ground black pepper

Preheat the oven to 350°F.

Set a wire rack on a rimmed baking sheet and put the tomatoes on the rack, cut sides up. Bake the tomatoes until the skin blisters, about 10 minutes. When cool enough to handle, peel and break into quarters with your hands.

Transfer the tomatoes and their juices to a blender, along with the shallot, garlic, celery, cucumber, bell pepper, and chile. Blend on low speed until pureed. Strain through a medium-mesh sieve into a bowl, pressing on the solids to extract as much liquid as possible. Season with the vinegar, salt, and sugar. Refrigerate until extremely cold.

Put the almonds in a small saucepan and add just enough olive oil to cover. Cook over medium heat until the almonds are fragrant and blonde, about 5 minutes. Remove from the heat, drain on paper towels, and let cool to room temperature. Reserve the almond cooking oil.

Divide the mozzarella, tomatoes, avocado, raspberries, basil, chile, and reserved almonds among cold soup bowls. Pour the soup into the bowls, drizzle with the almond cooking oil, and season with fleur de sel and pepper. Serve immediately.

c'est bon If you're in a hurry, you can set the bowl of soup in a larger bowl of ice and water to chill it quickly.

THIS WILL delight vegetarians—and carnivores, too. The warm, meaty mushrooms are so satisfying, especially when topped with pickled chiles, arugula, and Parmesan shavings. Fragrant fresh rosemary, which too often overpowers, adds a subtle depth of flavor to homemade mayonnaise, which is key here.

portobello parmesan sandwich with rosemary mayonnaise SERVES 4

2 tablespoons fresh lemon
  juice
1 tablespoon fresh rosemary
  leaves
1 large egg yolk
Kosher salt and freshly ground
  black pepper
¾ cup grapeseed or other
  neutral oil
¼ cup extra-virgin olive oil,
  plus more as needed
4 large portobello mushroom
  caps
4 kaiser rolls, split
Pickled Long Red Chiles
  (page 248), to taste
2 cups loosely packed arugula
  leaves
1-ounce block Parmigiano-
  Reggiano cheese

Set the oven rack 6 inches from the broiler heat source. Preheat the broiler to high.

Process the lemon juice, 1 tablespoon water, and the rosemary in a food processor until the rosemary is finely chopped. Strain through a fine-mesh sieve, pressing on the solids to extract as much liquid as possible, and return the liquid to the processor; discard the solids.

Add the egg yolk and ¾ teaspoon salt and process until smooth. With the machine running, add the oils in a steady stream and process until emulsified.

Arrange the mushrooms in a single layer on a rimmed baking sheet. Season both sides liberally with salt and pepper. Drizzle generously with olive oil, turning to coat. Turn the mushrooms gill side up and broil for 8 minutes, then flip and broil until tender, about 3 minutes longer. Cut each mushroom into 4 slices at an angle, keeping each cap together.

Toast the rolls and spread the rosemary mayonnaise on both cut sides of each roll. Arrange a mushroom, gill side up, on the bottom of each roll and top with chiles, then arugula. Use a vegetable peeler to shave the cheese directly onto the arugula. Cover with the roll tops, cut each sandwich in half, and serve immediately.

ONE WEEKEND in Waccabuc, I was looking for something to snack on. I smeared some garlic aïoli on grilled slices of bread and topped it with some crab. It hit the spot, so I decided to turn it into a complete sandwich with a little chile and herbs. This is a great use of fennel fronds, which usually end up in the trash. Dill works just as well, too.

open-faced crab sandwich SERVES 4

8 ounces picked peekytoe or lump crabmeat, picked over for bits of shell

¾ teaspoon finely chopped fresh long green (finger) chile

½ teaspoon finely chopped fresh fennel fronds or dill leaves

2 tablespoons extra-virgin olive oil, plus more for the bread

¼ teaspoon kosher salt

¼ teaspoon freshly ground black pepper

4 large (¾-inch-thick) slices artisan bread

Garlic Aïoli (page 245)

Lemon wedges, for serving

Preheat the broiler or grill to high.

Gently stir together the crab, chile, fennel fronds, oil, salt, and pepper in a medium bowl.

Drizzle olive oil all over the bread. Broil or grill until browned and crisp, turning to cook evenly.

Spread 2 tablespoons aïoli on each slice of bread and top with the crab mixture. Carefully cut each sandwich in half and serve with lemon wedges.

and croque madames all over France. My mom cooks the sandwiches in a cast-iron press on the stovetop so that the bread becomes a crisp casing for the filling. I prefer a sandwich that's hot and moist all the way through, so I bake the cheese on top of the bread and spread béchamel throughout. That's the key to my version: The bread must completely absorb the sauce. The effort is well worth it.

croque m   SERVES 4

BÉCHAMEL MORNAY

1½ cups whole milk
½ cup half-and-half
Kosher salt and freshly ground
    black pepper
Freshly grated nutmeg
3½ tablespoons unsalted butter
⅓ cup all-purpose flour
2 large egg yolks
1¼ ounces Gruyère, shredded
    (¼ cup)
1¼ ounces Comté, shredded
    (¼ cup)

SANDWICHES

8 slices Pullman bread, about
    6 inches square and ⅓ inch
    thick
5 ounces thinly sliced ham
3 ounces Comté, shredded
    (⅔ cup)
3 ounces Gruyère, shredded
    (⅔ cup)
Unsalted butter for the pan
8 quail eggs or 4 large eggs

Fleur de sel or other coarse sea
    salt
Cayenne pepper

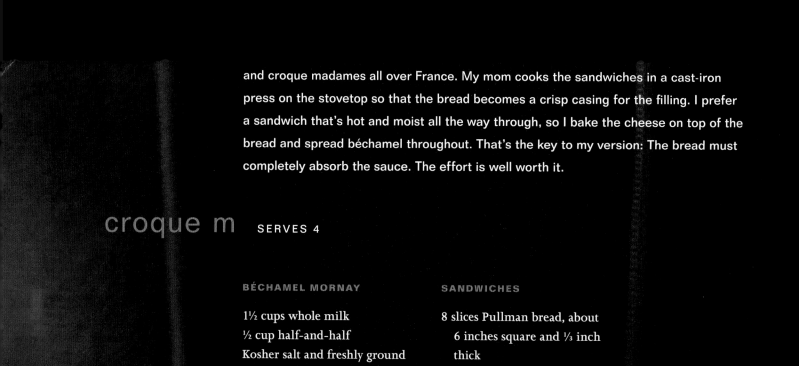

To make the béchamel, heat the milk, half-and-half, and a pinch each of salt, pepper, and nutmeg in a medium saucepan until bubbles begin to form. Keep warm over low heat.

In a large saucepan, melt the butter over medium-low heat until golden. Add the flour and cook, whisking constantly, until the mixture smells nutty and toasty, about 2 minutes. Continue whisking and add the hot milk mixture in a slow, steady stream. Bring the mixture to a boil while whisking. Remove from the heat.

In a small bowl, whisk the egg yolks until blended. Continue whisking and add a cup of the hot milk mixture in a slow, steady stream. Whisk the egg mixture back into the hot milk mixture until well blended. Cook over low heat, stirring constantly, until thickened. Add the cheeses and stir until melted. Season with more salt, pepper, and nutmeg to taste. It's easier to spread the sauce if refrigerated first in an airtight container until cold, but you can also use it right away.

To make the sandwiches, lay your bread slices in 2 rows of 4 to form a rectangle on a large sheet of parchment paper. The edges of the bread should be touching. Dollop 2 tablespoons béchamel onto each slice of bread. Use an offset spatula or the dull edge of a butter knife to push the sauce evenly into the bread, spreading back and forth repeatedly. This will take some time; you want the bread to completely soak up the sauce.

On the bottom row of bread, arrange the ham in an even layer. Dollop the remaining béchamel over the ham and spread evenly. Top with the remaining bread, béchamel side up. Sprinkle the cheeses evenly over the sandwiches and then press them into the bread.

Bring up the sides of parchment to enclose the sandwiches, then wrap tightly with plastic. Refrigerate until the sandwiches hold together nicely, at least 1 hour, but preferably 1 day. The longer the béchamel sits on the bread, the moister the sandwich will be.

Preheat the oven to 350°F. Butter a rimmed baking sheet.

Trim the crusts off the sandwiches, then slice each sandwich in half diagonally. Transfer to the prepared pan, spacing the sandwiches ½ inch apart. Bake until the cheeses melt and the tops are golden brown, about 10 minutes.

When the sandwiches are almost done, heat a large nonstick skillet over medium-high heat. Crack the eggs into the skillet, spacing them apart, and cook just until the whites are set, about 1 minute for quail eggs, longer for large eggs.

Slide the eggs on top of the sandwiches and sprinkle fleur de sel and cayenne on top. Serve immediately.

c'est bon To crack quail eggs, gently tap the sharp blade of a small knife against the equator of the egg. When it breaks through the shell, carefully twist the knife to split the shell in half.

I LIKE TO make my sandwiches more French than American, which is to say, I use less meat. Here, there's just enough turkey proportional to the other ingredients. Be sure to use high-quality roasted turkey here to best enjoy the bright, fresh mayonnaise. Of course, the best turkey option will come from your Thanksgiving leftovers (page 146).

turkey and bacon sandwich with arugula mayonnaise MAKES 4

1 large egg yolk

2 teaspoons Dijon mustard

Kosher salt and freshly ground black pepper

1 cup grapeseed or other neutral oil

2½ teaspoons fresh lemon juice

2 ounces arugula, sliced (1½ cups), plus 2 ounces whole arugula leaves (1¾ cups)

¾ cup fresh basil leaves, sliced

⅓ cup finely chopped fresh chives

4 large ciabatta rolls, split

1 pound sliced roasted turkey

8 slices good bacon, cooked until crisp

12 slices tomato (from about 3 tomatoes)

24 slices jarred pickled jalapeño

Whisk together the yolk, mustard, and ¼ teaspoon salt in a medium bowl until well blended. Continue whisking while adding the oil in a slow, steady stream to emulsify the mixture. Whisk in 2 teaspoons of the lemon juice until well blended.

Stir in the sliced arugula, basil, chives, and remaining ½ teaspoon lemon juice. Season to taste with salt and pepper.

Toast the ciabatta and spread a generous layer of the arugula mayonnaise on the cut sides. On the bottom of each roll, stack the turkey, whole arugula, bacon, tomato, and jalapeño. Cover with the roll tops, slice each sandwich in half, and serve immediately.

FOR FOUR generations, the Vongerichten family has been turning out this tart, which is like a quiche but creamier.

creamy onion tart SERVES 6

1 large white onion, very
   thinly sliced
4 tablespoons (½ stick)
   unsalted butter
Kosher salt and freshly ground
   black pepper
¼ cup all-purpose flour
¾ cup whole milk, warmed
⅓ cup heavy cream, warmed
2 large eggs, lightly beaten
Freshly grated nutmeg
½ recipe Pâte Brisée (page
   250), blind baked

Preheat the oven to 325°F.

In a large skillet, combine the onion, 2 tablespoons of the butter, and a generous pinch of salt. Cover and cook, stirring occasionally, over medium-low heat until very tender and pale gold, about 25 minutes.

In a large saucepan, melt the remaining 2 tablespoons butter over medium-low heat. Add the flour and cook, whisking constantly, until the mixture smells nutty, about 2 minutes. Whisk in the milk and cream in a slow, steady stream. Still whisking, bring to a boil and cook for 2 minutes. Remove from the heat and let cool slightly, whisking occasionally.

Whisk in the eggs, a little at a time, until well incorporated and smooth. Stir in the onion, then season to taste with salt, pepper, and nutmeg. Transfer the mixture to the tart shell, spreading it in an even layer.

Bake until golden brown and a knife inserted in the center comes out clean, about 1 hour. Let cool in the pan on a rack for 20 minutes. Unmold and serve warm.

I COULD EAT bowls and bowls of this. By blending a reduced cream mixture with a fresh one, this pasta tastes ultrarich and light at the same time. The best part of this dish: It's incredibly fast.

fettuccine with meyer lemon cream SERVES 4

Fresh Pasta Dough (page 249) or 8 ounces store-bought fresh fettuccine
Semolina flour, if using fresh dough
Kosher salt
1½ cups heavy cream
Grated zest of 2 Meyer lemons
2 tablespoons fresh Meyer lemon juice
2-ounce block Parmigiano-Reggiano cheese
Coarsely ground black pepper

If using dough, roll the dough through a pasta machine on each setting from widest to narrowest. Roll once more through the narrowest setting. Cut the dough into 12-inch-long sheets with a sharp knife, then pass the sheets through the fettuccine cutter. Toss with semolina flour to prevent sticking. You can cover the pasta with a damp paper towel, then plastic wrap, and refrigerate for up to 2 days.

Bring a large pot of water to a boil and salt it generously.

Meanwhile, whisk together the cream, lemon zest, and a pinch of salt. Pour 1 cup of the mixture into a large, deep skillet. Boil it rapidly, stirring frequently, until reduced by about half, about 8 minutes.

After the sauce has reduced for 5 minutes, cook the fettuccine in the water until al dente, about 3 minutes.

Drain the pasta well and add to the lemon cream. Reduce the heat to low and toss until well coated. Add the remaining cream mixture and the lemon juice and continue tossing until well coated.

Divide among 4 shallow bowls. Grate the cheese directly over the pasta, forming a little mound. Grind a generous dose of pepper over the pasta. Serve immediately.

THIS IS ONE of the most requested dishes in my home, especially when we have children over. Instead of making a béchamel sauce, Marja simply blends her ingredients and bakes them into a rich custard that suspends the pasta. Her blend of five cheeses creates layers of flavors in this homey casserole. Marja's always happy to bake it for a crowd, and everyone's always happy to eat it.

marja's mac 'n' cheese SERVES 12

Unsalted butter
1½ cups heavy cream
1½ cups half-and-half
⅔ cup whole milk
2 large eggs
2 large egg yolks
½ teaspoon freshly grated
  nutmeg
Kosher salt and freshly ground
  black pepper
6 ounces extra-sharp Cheddar
  cheese, shredded (1½ cups)
6 ounces sharp Cheddar
  cheese, shredded (1½ cups)
6 ounces mild yellow Cheddar
  cheese, shredded (1½ cups)
6 ounces Monterey Jack cheese,
  shredded (1½ cups)
1 pound dried elbow macaroni
4 ounces cream cheese, chilled,
  cut into small pieces

Preheat the oven to 350°F. Butter a 13 × 9 × 2-inch baking dish.

Whisk together the cream, half-and-half, milk, eggs, yolks, and nutmeg in a large bowl. Season with salt and pepper and whisk again. Combine the shredded cheeses in another large bowl and mix well.

Cook the macaroni in boiling salted water until almost al dente, about 3 minutes. The pasta should still be firm. Drain well.

Spoon a third of the macaroni into the buttered dish, and top with a third of the cheese mixture. Season with salt and pepper. Repeat layering and seasoning twice. Dot the surface with the cream cheese, then carefully pour the cream mixture into the dish.

Bake for 5 minutes, then use a large offset spatula or the back of a spoon to spread the melted cream cheese evenly over the top. Continue to bake until just set, about 40 minutes. Serve warm.

THIS PASTA DISH pairs creamy with crunchy, tart with sweet. Summer string beans also offer a little crunch to balance the juiciness of the tomatoes. I especially like using orange Sunbursts from my garden.

tagliatelle with pistachio pesto, string beans, and cherry tomatoes

SERVES 4

Fresh Pasta Dough (page 249) or 8 ounces store-bought fresh tagliatelle

Semolina flour, if using fresh dough

1 pint cherry tomatoes, halved

Kosher salt

1 small garlic clove, very thinly sliced

Extra-virgin olive oil

4 fresh basil leaves, torn, plus more for garnish

8 ounces green and/or wax beans, trimmed and cut into 1-inch pieces

Pistachio Pesto (recipe follows)

1-ounce block Parmigiano-Reggiano cheese

Freshly ground black pepper

If using dough, roll the dough through a pasta machine on each setting from widest to narrowest. Roll once more through the narrowest setting. Cut the dough into 12-inch-long sheets with a sharp knife, then pass the sheets through the tagliatelle cutter. Toss with semolina flour to prevent sticking. You can cover the pasta with a damp paper towel, then plastic wrap, and refrigerate for up to 2 days.

Preheat the oven to 200°F.

Arrange half of the tomatoes, cut sides up, on a small rimmed baking sheet. Season with salt, drizzle oil all over, and scatter the garlic and basil over the top. Bake until the tomato skins wrinkle a little, about 30 minutes. Discard the garlic and basil.

Bring a large pot of water to a boil and salt it generously. Fill a large bowl with ice and water. Cook the beans in the boiling water until crisp-tender, about 5 minutes. Use a slotted spoon to transfer to the ice water.

Add the tagliatelle to the boiling water and cook until al dente, about 3 minutes.

Meanwhile, coat a large skillet with olive oil and set over medium-low heat. Add the remaining fresh tomatoes, season with salt, and cook, tossing occasionally, until just warm. Remove from the heat and stir in the pesto and 2 tablespoons of the pasta cooking water.

Drain the pasta and beans and add to the skillet, along with the baked tomatoes. Toss gently to mix and then transfer to serving bowls. Tear basil over each serving. Grate the cheese directly over the pasta. Grind pepper over the cheese. Serve immediately.

pistachio pesto   MAKES ABOUT 1¼ CUPS

When basil grows in my garden, I want to make the most of it. To enhance its aroma, I pair it with pistachios and add a hit of chile and lemon zest to brighten it. Be sure to start with roasted pistachios in their shells and to keep the pesto coarse to highlight the crunch of the nuts.

3 cups packed fresh basil leaves
1 small garlic clove
1 fresh green Thai chile, stemmed,
   seeded, and chopped
8 (3-inch) strips fresh lemon zest
   (removed with a vegetable peeler)
1 cup extra-virgin olive oil
1 teaspoon kosher salt
1 cup shelled unsalted pistachios,
   lightly toasted
2 tablespoons freshly grated
   Parmigiano-Reggiano cheese

Bring a small saucepan of water to a boil. Fill a medium bowl with ice and water. Add the basil leaves to the boiling water, cook for 30 seconds, then drain and transfer to the ice water. When cool, drain well, then squeeze between sheets of paper towels until completely dry.

Put the basil in the blender along with the garlic, chile, lemon zest, oil, and salt. Puree until smooth. Add the pistachios and pulse until coarsely chopped. Transfer to a bowl and stir in the cheese.

MY TAKE ON linguine vongole includes a lot of vegetables for an added freshness. I also use clam juice, as well as the traditional wine, for a more complex sauce.

linguine with clams, chile, and parsley SERVES 4

Fresh Pasta Dough (page 249)
  or 8 ounces store-bought
  fresh linguine
Semolina flour, if using fresh
  dough
⅓ cup bottled clam juice
3 tablespoons dry white wine,
  such as Sauvignon Blanc
Kosher salt
3 tablespoons extra-virgin olive
  oil, plus more for drizzling
⅓ cup finely diced carrot
⅓ cup finely diced leek, white
  and pale green parts only

¼ cup finely diced celery
1 tablespoon minced garlic
¼ teaspoon minced fresh red
  Thai chile
4 dozen littleneck clams (about
  5 pounds), well scrubbed
1 teaspoon crushed red chile
  flakes, ground finely in a
  spice grinder, or ⅛ teaspoon
  cayenne pepper
¼ cup fresh flat-leaf parsley
  leaves, thinly sliced

If using dough, roll the dough through a pasta machine on each setting from widest to narrowest. Roll once more through the narrowest setting. Cut the dough into 12-inch-long sheets with a sharp knife, then pass the sheets through the linguine cutter. Toss with semolina flour to prevent sticking. You can cover the pasta with a damp paper towel, then plastic wrap, and refrigerate for up to 2 days.

Stir together the clam juice and wine. Bring a large pot of water to a boil and salt it generously.

Heat the oil in a large sauté pan with a lid over medium-high heat. Add the carrot, leek, celery, garlic, chile, and a pinch of salt. Cook, stirring, until golden, about 4 minutes. Add the clams and clam juice mixture, cover, and cook, shaking the pan occasionally, just until the clams open, about 5 minutes.

Meanwhile, add the linguine to the boiling water and cook until al dente, about 3 minutes. Drain and add to the clam mixture. Cook, tossing gently, until the pasta is glazed with the sauce.

Transfer to shallow serving bowls and sprinkle the ground chile all over. Garnish with the parsley and serve immediately.

FRESH SPINACH and cheese is one of my favorite combinations. Here, the blast of the heat from the oven wilts the greens into the melted cheese. To brighten the flavors, I toss in a bunch of fresh herbs, too. If you have a pizza oven or stone at home, use it here. It'll char the edges of the leaves and make them crisp.

herbed spinach and three-cheese pizza MAKES 4 INDIVIDUAL PIZZAS

Semolina flour

Pizza Dough (page 250),
   divided into 4 balls

8 ounces Comté or Gruyère
   cheese, diced (1½ cups)

¾ cup freshly grated
   Parmigiano-Reggiano cheese

8 ounces fresh ricotta (1 cup)

18 ounces spinach leaves
   (6 cups)

1⅓ cups loosely packed fresh
   dill sprigs and basil leaves

Extra-virgin olive oil

Kosher salt and freshly ground
   black pepper

Put a pizza stone on the lowest oven rack. Preheat the oven to 500°F. Let the stone get very, very hot.

Sprinkle a baking sheet with semolina flour. Pick up a dough ball with your fingers and gently pinch the edges of the ball while rotating it so that the dough stretches into a round. Drape the round over your knuckles and continue turning and stretching until the center is so thin it's almost translucent. The dough should be about 9 inches in diameter. Gently place on the prepared sheet. Unless you have a very large pizza stone or baking sheet, you can probably make only 1 or 2 pizzas at a time. Keep the other dough rounds covered with plastic wrap until ready to use.

Spread a quarter of the Comté and Parmesan on the dough round, then crumble a quarter of the ricotta over the top. Scatter a quarter of the spinach and herbs over the cheese. Drizzle a little oil all over and season with salt. Slide the sheet onto the hot stone and bake until the crust is browned and crisp, the cheese is melted, and the spinach is wilted, about 10 minutes. Grind pepper all over. Repeat with the remaining ingredients, serving each pizza hot as it comes out of the oven.

WHEN I WAS a kid, one of my favorite fall activities was hunting for wild mushrooms with my brothers in the woods around our home. For this pizza, make sure the mushroom pieces are all roughly the same size so they cook evenly. The runny egg yolk that sauces this pizza binds all the flavors together.

mixed wild mushroom pizza with fried eggs   MAKES 4 INDIVIDUAL PIZZAS

½ cup extra-virgin olive oil, plus more as needed

2 garlic cloves, finely minced

Semolina flour

Pizza Dough (page 250), divided into 4 balls

1 cup freshly grated Parmigiano-Reggiano cheese

12 ounces fontina, diced (2¼ cups)

12 ounces fresh ricotta (1½ cups)

4 cups mixed fresh wild mushrooms, such as oyster, king oyster, shiitake, cremini, enoki, and chanterelle, thinly sliced

¼ cup thinly sliced fresh morels

Kosher salt and freshly ground black pepper

4 large eggs

Put a pizza stone or baking sheet on the lowest oven rack. Preheat the oven to 500°F. Let the stone get very, very hot.

In a small bowl, combine the oil and garlic.

Form the dough balls as for Herbed Spinach and Three-Cheese Pizza (opposite).

Spread a quarter of the Parmesan and fontina on the dough round, then crumble a quarter of the ricotta over the top. Scatter a quarter of the mushrooms over the cheese. Drizzle a quarter of the garlic oil all over the pizza and season with salt. Slide the sheet onto the hot stone and bake until the crust is browned and crisp, the cheese is melted, and the mushrooms are tender, about 15 minutes.

While the pizza bakes, heat a little oil in a small non-stick skillet over medium heat. Crack 1 egg into the skillet, lightly season with salt and pepper, and cook, sunny side up, until the white is just set and the yolk is runny.

Grind pepper all over the pizza and slide the egg onto the pie. Repeat with the remaining ingredients, serving each pizza hot as it comes out of the oven.

sausage and kale pizza

MAKES 4 INDIVIDUAL PIZZAS

1¼ cups canned San Marzano
    tomatoes (from one
    14.5-ounce can)

Extra-virgin olive oil

Kosher salt

Semolina flour

Pizza Dough (page 250),
    divided into 4 balls

12 ounces fresh ricotta
    (1½ cups)

½ cup freshly grated pecorino
    Romano cheese

8 to 10 ounces Italian sausage
    links, removed from casing
    and broken into ½-inch
    pieces

1 cup very thinly sliced kale
    leaves

Freshly ground black pepper

Set a fine-mesh sieve over a large bowl. Peel the tomatoes if necessary and remove the green cores. Use your hands to completely crush the tomatoes over the sieve, then let the crushed tomatoes stand in the sieve for 1 hour to drain the juices; reserve the juices for another use.

Put a pizza stone on the lowest oven rack. Preheat the oven to 500°F. Let the stone get very, very hot.

Transfer the crushed tomatoes to a bowl and stir in 1 teaspoon oil and ¼ teaspoon salt.

Sprinkle a baking sheet with semolina flour. Pick up a dough ball with your fingers and gently pinch the edges of the ball while rotating it so that the dough stretches into a round. Drape the round over your knuckles and continue turning and stretching until the center is so thin it's almost translucent. The dough should be 9 inches in diameter. Gently place on the prepared sheet. Unless you have a very large pizza stone, you can probably make only 1 or 2 pizzas at a time. Keep the other dough rounds covered with plastic wrap until ready to use.

Spread a quarter of the tomato sauce over the dough, leaving a ½-inch rim. Dollop a quarter of the ricotta evenly on the sauce, scatter a quarter of the pecorino and a quarter of the sausage pieces over the dough, then top with a quarter of the kale. Drizzle with oil, season with salt, and slide the pizza onto the hot stone. Bake until the crust is browned and crisp, the sausage is cooked through, and the kale is wilted, about 15 minutes. Grind pepper all over the pizza. Repeat with the remaining ingredients, serving each pizza hot as it comes out of the oven.

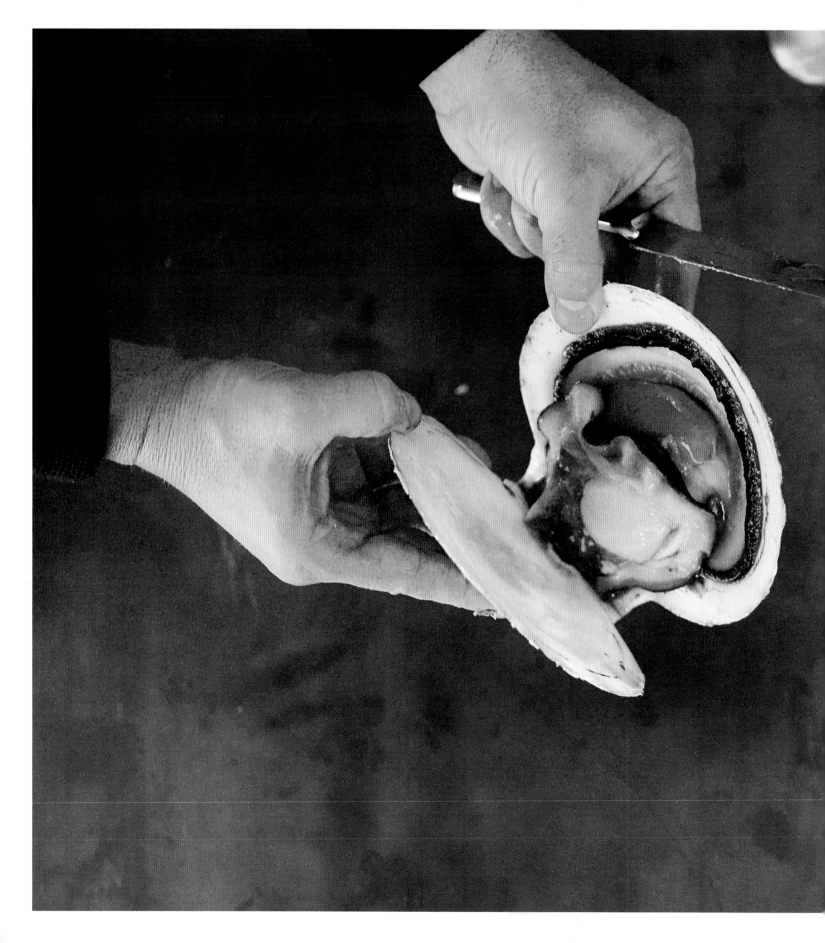

fish and seafood

I WANT MY FISH DISHES TO REALLY excite. Fish is often quite subtle in flavor and delicate in texture. But I want thrilling dishes that wow. Starting with the fish and shellfish as a platform—always the freshest possible—I create strong flavors for them to stand up against. I don't want to overpower the fish, but I do want to push the seasonings to the limit. There's a point at which the sauces and accompaniments I create for the fish bring it to life. The effect should be something like fireworks. It's a careful balancing act of seeing how much the fish can take before its natural flavor is lost in the mix. The first bite should be as memorable as the last.

That isn't to say you have to use only the fish I specify in the recipes that follow. You should use whatever fresh, sustainable fish you can find locally. Even though my home is in New York, I spend much of the year traveling to my restaurants around the world and using the fish and seafood in each region. As long as you use the same type of fish (white, oily, flaky, etc.), you'll get great results. If you don't know where to find fresh seafood, you can try out my favorite purveyors: Blue Ribbon for shrimp and bass; Browne Trading for cod and arctic char; Pierless for squid, turbot, and snapper; scallops from Day Boat Collective; and crab from Morningstar.

When you make these dishes, be sure to taste as you go. You should always be able to still taste the fish and be thrilled by the intensity of the dish. When the flavors all come together, it's magic.

ANY FISH on the bone works here—whole red snapper or salmon steaks would also be good choices—but I especially love just-caught sea bass. Set on a bed of fennel and smothered with tart-sweet Meyer lemons and cherry tomatoes, the fish absorbs all those flavors while it steam-roasts in dry white wine. I love the distinctive citrus aroma of Meyer lemons, but you can use regular lemons here, too.

roasted whole sea bass with fennel, meyer lemons, and cherry tomatoes SERVES 4

Extra-virgin olive oil

2 fennel bulbs, cored and sliced paper-thin

2 teaspoons fennel seeds

Kosher salt and freshly ground black pepper

1 whole black sea bass (about 4 pounds), gutted and scaled

1 pint cherry tomatoes, halved

2 Meyer lemons, cut into very thin slices

½ cup chopped fresh flat-leaf parsley leaves

1 cup dry white wine

Preheat the oven to 400°F.

Coat the bottom of a large roasting pan with oil. Arrange the fennel in an even layer to cover the bottom of the pan. Sprinkle the fennel seeds over the fennel and season with salt and pepper.

Center the fish on top. Season the fish inside and out with salt and pepper. Scatter the tomatoes around the fish. Cover the fish with the lemon slices and parsley. Pour the wine around the fish and season everything with salt and pepper.

Roast until a knife pierces through the flesh of the fish with no resistance and the blade feels warm, about 30 minutes. Remove from the oven and let rest for 10 minutes. Serve at the table.

THIS BROTH IS so good I could drink it by the bowlful. Be sure to serve this with steamed sticky rice. Even better: When I have leftover sticky rice, I press it into small cubes and fry them until crisp and golden brown. You can find konbu, bonito, miso, and yuzu at a Japanese grocery or a well-stocked Asian market.

slow-cooked salmon in miso-yuzu broth SERVES 4

Unsalted butter

1 (3 × 4-inch) sheet konbu (see Pantry, page 253)

1 cup chicken stock, preferably homemade

1 fresh green Thai chile

⅓ cup bonito flakes

3 sprigs fresh dill

¼ cup white (shiro) miso (see Pantry, page 253)

1 tablespoon plus 1 teaspoon unsalted yuzu juice (see Pantry, page 253)

4 (6-ounce) boneless center-cut salmon fillets, skin on

Kosher salt and freshly ground black pepper

4 ounces silken tofu, diced

1-inch piece fresh ginger, peeled and finely julienned

1 scallion, white and green parts, thinly sliced at an angle

8 cherry tomatoes, halved

1 tablespoon fresh basil leaves

Preheat the oven to 300°F. Butter a large rimmed baking sheet.

Put the konbu on a small baking sheet and bake until dry and brittle, about 8 minutes. It should smell smoky.

Combine the konbu, chicken stock, and 1 cup water in a large saucepan. Cut the chile in half and add half to the pan. Bring to a simmer, then drop in the bonito. Crush the dill with your hands and stir into the mixture. Remove from the heat, cover, and let steep for 15 minutes. Strain through a fine-mesh sieve into a bowl, pressing on the solids to extract as much liquid as possible; discard the solids.

Mince the remaining chile half and set aside.

In a small bowl, stir together the miso and 1 cup of the broth until smooth. Return to the saucepan, along with the yuzu juice and remaining broth, and heat just until bubbles form. Do not let the mixture boil.

Meanwhile, season the salmon with salt and pepper and place on the prepared baking sheet, skin side up. Bake until the salmon skin peels off easily and a thin-bladed knife slides through the side of the fish against the grain with no resistance, about 12 minutes. Remove the skin from each fillet, carefully flip, and transfer to shallow bowls.

Divide the tofu, ginger, scallion, and tomatoes among the bowls, scattering them around the fish. Spoon the broth over each serving, garnish with basil and minced chile, and serve.

BARBECUE SAUCE, especially a spicy one, may seem an unusual pairing for fish, but the richness of salmon not only stands up to the heat, it actually is enhanced by the flavor of the sauce.

grilled salmon with cherry tomato barbecue sauce SERVES 4

2 pints cherry tomatoes, preferably Sunburst, halved
Kosher salt
¼ cup Barbecue Sauce (page 247), or to taste, warmed
4 (6-ounce) skinless, boneless center-cut salmon fillets, patted dry
Freshly ground black pepper
Extra-virgin olive oil
Fleur de sel or other coarse sea salt

Preheat the oven to 200°F.

Arrange the tomatoes, cut sides up, in a single layer on a rimmed baking sheet lined with parchment paper. Sprinkle a little kosher salt all over. Bake until the tomatoes have concentrated their flavor (the skins will wrinkle a little) but are not dry, about 30 minutes.

Transfer the tomatoes to a bowl and add the sauce. Gently toss until the tomatoes are evenly coated, adding more sauce if you like. Let stand for 15 minutes.

Heat your grill or a grill pan to medium-high.

Season the salmon on both sides with salt and pepper, then drizzle a little oil all over. Put on the grill, flat side down, and cook until the flesh releases easily from the grill grate, about 4 minutes. Carefully flip and cook until a thin-bladed knife slides through the side of the fish against the grain with no resistance, about 2 minutes longer.

Transfer the salmon to plates, spoon the sauce over the salmon, sprinkle with fleur de sel, and serve.

c'est bon To concentrate the flavor of your tomatoes, you can use the technique above or, if you have a gas oven, you can put the tray of tomatoes in the oven overnight. Leave the oven off; the heat from the pilot light alone will have the same effect.

SUPER-SAVORY green olives form the base of an amazing vinaigrette that brings out the sweetness of snapper and late-summer corn and potatoes.

red snapper, corn, and baby potatoes with green olive vinaigrette SERVES 4

½ cup thinly sliced pitted Cerignola olives (from 8 large olives)

2 tablespoons minced shallots

1 tablespoon capers, rinsed well and drained

2 teaspoons finely chopped jalapeño

2 tablespoons fresh lemon juice

1 tablespoon plus 1 teaspoon fresh lime juice

1 tablespoon plus 1 teaspoon champagne vinegar

7 tablespoons extra-virgin olive oil, plus more for cooking

Kosher salt

4 (6-ounce) skin-on, boneless red snapper fillets

Cayenne pepper

2½ cups fresh corn kernels (from 6 ears)

Herbed New Baby Potatoes (page 185)

Freshly ground black pepper

¼ cup finely chopped fresh herb leaves, preferably a mix of basil, chervil, chives, and mint, plus more for garnish

c'est bon To prevent the fish from sticking to the pan, be sure to dry the skin thoroughly first. To keep the skin dry, season at the very last minute, while the oil is heating. Over time, the salt draws moisture out of the fish and will cause the oil to splatter and the fish to stick. If the fish is stuck to the pan after cooking, add ½ teaspoon butter to the hot pan. Swirl it around so that it runs under the fish, and the fish should release.

Preheat the oven to 450°F.

To make the vinaigrette, combine the olives, shallots, capers, jalapeño, lemon juice, lime juice, vinegar, 5 tablespoons of the oil, and a pinch of salt. The flavors will get better as the vinaigrette sits. You can refrigerate it for up to 1 day.

Heat a large ovenproof skillet over high heat until very hot. Cut 3 diagonal slits in the skin of each fish fillet. Season the fish on both sides with salt and a pinch of cayenne. Coat the hot skillet with oil. When it's almost smoking, add the fish, skin side down. Cook until the skin is golden, about 4 minutes, then transfer to the oven. Cook just until a knife pierces through the flesh with little resistance, about 3 minutes.

Meanwhile, heat 2 tablespoons of the oil in another large skillet over medium-high heat. Add the corn and season with salt. Cook, stirring frequently, until golden and tender, about 6 minutes. Add the potatoes and cook for 1 minute longer to heat through. Season to taste with salt and pepper.

Spoon the corn mixture onto a serving dish and top with the fish, skin side up. Stir the herbs into the vinaigrette, then spoon over everything. Garnish with more herbs. Serve immediately.

herbed sea bass and potatoes in broth   SERVES 4

3 sprigs fresh rosemary, chopped

1 small bunch fresh thyme (½ ounce), chopped

2 (3-inch) strips fresh lemon zest (removed with a vegetable peeler), thinly sliced

1 tablespoon finely chopped peeled fresh ginger

Kosher salt

2 large Yukon Gold potatoes, cut into ½-inch chunks

1 small serrano chile

2 tablespoons finely chopped fresh mint leaves

2 tablespoons finely chopped fresh basil leaves

2 tablespoons finely chopped fresh dill

1 tablespoon finely chopped fresh marjoram leaves

4 (6- to 8-ounce) black sea bass fillets, skin on

3 tablespoons extra-virgin olive oil

6 ounces baby spinach

Lemon wedges, for serving

Blend the rosemary, thyme, and 4½ cups water in a blender until the herbs are finely ground. Strain through a fine-mesh sieve into a large saucepan, pressing on the herbs to extract as much liquid as possible; discard the solids. Add the zest, ginger, 1 tablespoon salt, and the potatoes to the pan. Bring to a boil, then reduce the heat to maintain a steady simmer. Cook until a knife easily pierces a potato, about 20 minutes.

Thinly slice a quarter of the chile and set aside. Remove the stem and seeds from the remaining chile and chop finely. Combine the chopped chile with the mint, basil, dill, and marjoram in a small bowl. Cut three ½-inch-deep slits crosswise in each fillet. Stuff ½ teaspoon of the herb mixture in each slit, being careful to not get it on the skin. Season the fish with salt.

Heat half of the oil in a large skillet over medium-high heat until almost smoking. Add 2 fillets, skin side down, and cook until golden brown and crisp, about 3 minutes. Carefully flip and cook until the fish is just cooked through, about 6 minutes longer. Transfer to a warm plate. Repeat with the remaining oil and fillets.

Add the spinach and sliced chile to the potatoes and broth. Cook, stirring, until the spinach just wilts. Divide the potato mixture and broth among shallow bowls. Top with the fish and season with a little salt. Serve with lemon.

I THINK tomatoes and summer squash always taste great together. The key to this two-vegetable simple spin on ratatouille is roasting the tomatoes first. It intensifies their sweetness and makes the whole dish rich in flavor.

cod with roasted tomatoes and summer squash SERVES 4

3 large ripe beefsteak tomatoes, cored and cut in half through their equators

Kosher salt and freshly ground black pepper

⅓ cup plus 5 tablespoons extra-virgin olive oil, plus more for cooking as needed

2 medium yellow squash, sliced 1 inch thick at an angle

¼ teaspoon crushed red chile flakes

¼ cup minced red onion

1 large garlic clove, minced

¼ fresh long red (finger) chile, minced, or more to taste

1 teaspoon minced fresh rosemary leaves

4 (6-ounce) skinless, boneless cod fillets

Wondra flour, for dusting

½ cup finely chopped fresh herb leaves, preferably a mix of basil, chives, and flat-leaf parsley

Preheat the oven to 250°F. Set a wire rack on a rimmed baking sheet.

Season the tomatoes with salt and pepper and drizzle with oil. Arrange on the rack, cut sides up. Bake until shriveled around the edges (but not dry), about 35 minutes. Cool, then peel and chop, reserving all of the flesh and juices.

Raise the oven temperature to 400°F.

Toss the squash with the chile flakes, 2 tablespoons of the oil, and a pinch of salt. Spread on a rimmed baking sheet. Roast until golden brown, about 17 minutes.

Meanwhile, heat ⅓ cup of the oil in a medium saucepan over medium-high heat. Add the onion and garlic and season with salt. Cook until golden, about 5 minutes. Add the chile, rosemary, and tomatoes and their juices and simmer for 6 minutes. Fold in the roasted squash and simmer for 2 minutes longer. Keep warm.

Heat a large ovenproof skillet over high heat until hot. Season the cod with salt and pepper and dust with Wondra. Coat the skillet with oil. When it's almost smoking, add the cod. Cook for 1 minute, then transfer to the oven. Cook until a knife pierces easily through the flesh, about 5 minutes.

Stir together the herbs and 3 tablespoons of the oil. Season with salt. Divide the tomato-squash stew among 4 shallow bowls. Place a fillet on top and spoon the herb oil over the fish. Serve immediately.

c'est bon Wondra is a superfine flour most commonly used to thicken gravy. I find that it does wonders for getting a thin, crisp golden brown crust on fish.

THERE ARE FEW things better than a good Maine lobster. With this technique, I preserve the taste of the sea by cooking the meat in its own juices. The secret? Cut the lobsters in half and balance the shells so that they capture all of the cooking juices. If you have a wood-burning oven, now is the time to use it.

roasted lobster with oregano and chile SERVES 4

4 live lobsters (each 1¼ to
   1½ pounds)
4 sprigs fresh oregano or
   ½ teaspoon dried oregano
¼ teaspoon crushed red chile
   flakes, or to taste
Maldon salt or other flaky
   sea salt
2 tablespoons fresh lemon
   juice
¾ cup extra-virgin olive oil
Lemon wedges, for serving

Preheat the oven to 450°F or heat your grill to high.

Bring a large pot of water to a boil. Fill a large bowl with ice and water. Plunge the lobsters into the boiling water until submerged. Boil for 1 minute, then remove from the pot. Keep the water boiling. Remove the claws from the lobsters, using oven mitts or a kitchen towel if too hot to handle. Plunge the lobster bodies into the ice bath. Return the large claws to the boiling water and cook for 2 minutes. Add the small claws and cook them all together for 2 minutes. Transfer all the claws to the ice bath and remove when cold.

Cut the lobster bodies in half down the center with kitchen shears. Remove the egg sacs, if present. Crack the lobster claws and remove one side of the shells, so that the meat is exposed on one side and cradled in the shell on the other. If roasting in the oven, arrange the lobsters and claws, shell side down, in a large roasting pan. Make sure the lobsters are lying flat so that the shells keep in the seasonings and juices, which will baste the meat while it's cooking.

If using fresh oregano, microwave it in 30-second intervals until dry and brittle, about 1½ minutes total. Strip the leaves from the stems and crumble the oregano—fresh or dried—over the lobsters. Sprinkle the chile flakes all over, season with salt, and then drizzle with the lemon juice and oil.

Roast the lobsters in the oven or balance on the grill grate and grill until aromatic and the meat becomes opaque, about 15 minutes. Serve immediately with lemon wedges.

c'est bon When I started cooking at home, I began using the microwave a lot more. I discovered that it's great for making your own dried herbs. Just microwave in short intervals until brittle and fragrant. They're fresher and more flavorful than the bottled stuff at the store.

AT THE HEIGHT of summer, I'm always thinking of new ways to combine farmer's market vegetables. Eggplants and peppers are a natural pair, and I like to highlight their different textures here. I roast the eggplants until they almost collapse, but quick-char the peppers to keep their crunch while giving them a smoky flavor. Perfectly seared scallops tie the two textures and flavors together.

seared scallops with roasted eggplants and marinated peppers

SERVES 4

4 small Japanese eggplants (about 12 ounces total)

¼ teaspoon minced garlic

2 tablespoons fresh lemon juice

3 tablespoons extra-virgin olive oil, plus more as needed

Crushed red chile flakes

Kosher salt and freshly ground black pepper

1 red bell pepper

1 orange bell pepper

2 tablespoons fresh lime juice

12 large sea scallops (1 pound), patted dry

Fresh dill leaves

Arrange the oven rack in the lowest position. Preheat the oven to 450°F.

Use a fork to poke holes all over the eggplants. Put the eggplants on a foil-lined baking sheet in the oven. Roast, turning occasionally, until the skins are charred and the eggplants are very soft, about 15 minutes. Transfer to a cutting board.

When cool enough to handle, peel the eggplants and cut in quarters lengthwise. Cut each piece in half cross-wise. Transfer to a large bowl. Add the garlic, lemon juice, 2 tablespoons of the oil, a pinch of chile flakes, and a pinch of salt. Gently stir well.

Turn a gas burner to high. Set the peppers directly over the flame and cook, turning frequently, until the skin is charred all over. Alternatively, broil or grill the peppers as close to the heat source as possible. When cool enough to handle, use paper towels to rub off the charred skin. Remove and discard the stems and seeds, then cut each pepper into very thin slices. Transfer to a medium bowl and add the lime juice, remaining 1 tablespoon oil, and a pinch of salt. Stir well.

Heat a large skillet over high heat until very hot. Season half the scallops with salt and pepper. Add enough oil to generously coat the bottom of the pan, then add the seasoned scallops, one at a time. Cook until a golden brown crust forms on the bottom, 1 to 2 minutes, then carefully flip and cook until a crust forms on the other side, 1 to 2 minutes longer. Transfer to paper towels to drain. Repeat with the remaining scallops in the same pan, letting the pan get very hot again and adding more oil if needed.

Divide the eggplant mixture among 4 serving dishes. Top with the scallops, then the pepper mixture. Scatter the dill all over.

crab cakes with gingered grapefruit and avocado

SERVES 4 TO 6 AS A MAIN COURSE; 12 AS A FIRST COURSE

1 pink grapefruit

¼ cup Ginger Syrup (page 244)

1 large egg yolk

4½ teaspoons Colman's dry mustard

1½ teaspoons kosher salt

1 teaspoon finely ground celery seeds

3 tablespoons fresh lemon juice

¾ teaspoon green Tabasco sauce

½ teaspoon red Tabasco sauce

½ teaspoon Worcestershire sauce

¾ cup grapeseed or other neutral oil, plus more for frying

1½ pounds picked peekytoe or lump crabmeat, picked over for bits of shell

4 slices good white bread, crusts removed and cut into ½-inch cubes (2¼ cups)

2 tablespoons Wondra flour

1 avocado, halved, pitted, peeled, and thinly sliced

Use a sharp knife to trim the top and bottom from the grapefruit, then cut off the peel and pith. Holding the grapefruit over a medium bowl, slice between the membranes to release the grapefruit segments into the bowl. Pour the ginger syrup over the grapefruit. Let stand while you prepare the crab cakes.

Whisk together the yolk, mustard, salt, celery seeds, lemon juice, both Tabasco sauces, and Worcestershire sauce in a large bowl. Continue whisking while adding the oil in a slow, steady stream to emulsify the mixture. Gently fold in the crab and bread.

Form the mixture into twelve 3-inch-round patties and dust with Wondra. Coat a large nonstick pan with oil and heat over medium heat until shimmering. Add 4 patties to the pan and cook until golden brown on both sides, about 6 minutes total, carefully turning once. Drain on paper towels. Repeat with the remaining patties, wiping out the pan and adding and heating more oil between batches.

Divide the avocado slices among serving plates. Spoon the grapefruit and its syrup all around and place the crab cakes on top.

COLD SOUP and hot shrimp—this is a fantastic combination on a warm night. Blending the honeyed sweetness of this summer melon with intensely savory vegetables makes this dish incredibly refreshing. And I give the hot, spicy shrimp a hit of freshness by grilling finely sliced mint right onto them.

fiery grilled shrimp with honeydew gazpacho SERVES 4

½ ripe honeydew, seeded
1 small fennel bulb, coarsely chopped
1 celery heart stalk, coarsely chopped
½ English cucumber, peeled and coarsely chopped
2 jalapeños, stemmed, seeded, and chopped
1 fresh green Thai chile, stemmed, seeded, and minced
3 tablespoons fresh lime juice, plus more to taste and wedges for serving

1 tablespoon kosher salt, plus more to taste
1 teaspoon sugar, plus more to taste
Crushed red chile flakes
¼ cup packed fresh mint leaves, very thinly sliced, plus more for garnish
1 pound large (16- to 20-count) shrimp, shelled and deveined
Extra-virgin olive oil

Cut away the honeydew rind and the dark green flesh close to the rind. Cut the honeydew into 1-inch chunks. You should have 4 cups of melon.

Put the melon in a blender along with the fennel, celery, cucumber, and jalapeños. Blend on low speed until almost smooth. Strain through a medium-mesh sieve, pressing on the solids to extract as much liquid as possible; discard the solids. Stir in the minced chile, lime juice, salt, and sugar. Taste and adjust seasonings. Cover tightly and refrigerate until very cold.

When ready to serve, heat your grill on high until very hot.

Sprinkle salt, chile flakes, and the mint all over the shrimp, then gently press in the seasonings. Drizzle a little oil all over the shrimp. Grill the shrimp, flipping once, until just opaque throughout, about 3 minutes. Skewer to serve if desired.

Divide the cold soup among cold serving bowls. Serve the hot shrimp on small plates next to the bowls. Drizzle a little oil over the soup and shrimp. Garnish the soup with mint and squirt a little lime juice over the shrimp. Serve immediately.

c'est bon To keep shrimp moist and juicy while getting lightly browned in the broiler, I add a splash of water to the pan. Think of it as steam-broiling.

THE BEAUTY OF this dish is the butter and soy combination. I dress a fresh green salad with a light, lemony soy sauce vinaigrette, then top it with shrimp coated in a creamy beurre blanc. To marry the two elements, I use champagne vinegar in place of the traditional white wine for a sharper beurre blanc.

shrimp salad with champagne beurre blanc SERVES 4

4 tablespoons (½ stick) unsalted butter, softened, plus more for the pan

1 cup champagne vinegar

2 tablespoons minced shallots

⅓ cup heavy cream

Kosher salt

Cayenne pepper

20 large (16- to 20-count) shrimp, shelled and deveined

12 ounces mixed greens (about 8 cups)

½ cup peeled, diced fresh tomatoes

2 avocados, halved, pitted, peeled, and thinly sliced

4 large white mushroom caps, thinly sliced

House Dressing (page 245)

2 tablespoons snipped chives, for garnish

Arrange an oven rack 4 inches from the broiler heat source. Preheat the broiler. Generously butter a rimmed baking sheet.

In a small saucepan, combine the vinegar and shallots. Boil over high heat, stirring occasionally, until the liquid has almost completely evaporated and the shallots are glazed, 12 to 15 minutes.

Stir in the cream and continue boiling until reduced by half, about 2 minutes. Reduce the heat to low and whisk in the butter, a little at a time, until well incorporated. Season to taste with salt and cayenne.

Meanwhile, butterfly the shrimp by cutting each in half along its vein, slicing all the way through the curved middle, but keeping the stubby ends connected. Open the butterflied shrimp (they'll resemble hearts) and arrange in the prepared pan in a single layer. Season with salt and cayenne, then splash a little water over the shrimp. Broil until the shrimp just become opaque, about 3 minutes.

Divide the greens among serving dishes. Arrange the tomatoes and avocados over the greens, then scatter the mushrooms all around. Spoon the dressing all over. Arrange the shrimp around the center and spoon the beurre blanc over the shrimp. Garnish with chives.

WITH BOTH fennel seeds and fresh fennel, you get an intensely fragrant dish. I can't think of a simpler or faster dinner. With good crusty bread for soaking up the juices and a simple salad, you're all set. Look for small Prince Edward Island mussels—they're my favorite.

mussels with fennel duo   SERVES 4

1 tablespoon fennel seeds

2 tablespoons extra-virgin
  olive oil

2 tablespoons unsalted butter

1 cup thinly sliced fennel
  (from 1 large or 2 small
  bulbs)

Kosher salt

2 (3-inch-long) strips lemon
  zest (removed with a
  vegetable peeler)

4 pounds mussels, beards
  trimmed, washed well

½ cup dry white wine, such as
  Sauvignon Blanc

¼ cup loosely packed fresh
  basil leaves

In a large, wide pot that can comfortably hold the mussels, toast the fennel seeds over medium-high heat until fragrant. Add the oil, butter, fennel, and a pinch of salt. Raise the heat to high and cook until the mixture is bubbling and fragrant, about 2 minutes. Stir in the lemon zest.

Add the mussels and wine and cover. Cook, shaking the pot occasionally, just until the mussels open, about 10 minutes. Toss in the basil leaves.

Divide the mussels and all of their cooking liquid among serving bowls.

IMAGINE EATING mussels in their purest form. One bite of this dish and you'll feel like you're at sea. Quickly steamed in a rich seaweed broth, the mussels here are simply amazing. Sticky rice is great for soaking up the sauce, although I also like slurping it straight from the mussel shells.

mussels in konbu broth   SERVES 4

1 (4 × 2-inch) sheet konbu
   (see Pantry, page 253)
2 tablespoons extra-virgin
   olive oil
2 tablespoons unsalted butter
2 medium shallots, minced
Kosher salt
4 pounds mussels, beards
   trimmed, washed well
½ cup dry white wine, such as
   Sauvignon Blanc

Soak the konbu in hot water until softened and pliable, about 2 minutes. Drain well, pat dry, then julienne.

In a large, wide pot that can comfortably hold the mussels, combine the oil, butter, shallots, konbu, and a pinch of salt. Cook over medium-high heat until the butter melts and the mixture is fragrant, about 1 minute.

Add the mussels and wine, cover, and raise the heat to high. Cook, shaking the pot occasionally, just until the mussels open, about 10 minutes.

Divide the mussels and all of their cooking liquid among serving bowls.

poultry

MANY MAY THINK OF CHICKEN AS a boring weeknight default dish, but I consider a juicy, well-cooked bird one of life's great pleasures. Growing up, we only had poultry a few times a month, so I still think of it as a treat. Chicken parts are big in America—and undeniably convenient—but I've always preferred starting with a whole bird, even if I am going to cut it up. Air-chilled, free-range birds are best, as are smaller birds. They're hard to find, but they're tastier and more tender than larger ones.

Chicken is the perfect canvas for introducing new flavors that everyone in the family will like. At home, I don't cook just for myself; I cook for my family. And, yes, there are some picky kids. But I don't do chicken nuggets. Instead, I crust chicken breasts with a crisp, savory Parmesan coating. Everyone—kids and adults—asks for this dish now.

Duck, on the other hand, feels like a special occasion dish—and for good reason. Its rich meat makes you feel like celebrating. That said, it made regular appearances in our repertoire at home in France— usually whole. My mom strained and saved the leftover fat, using it to cook potatoes or make confits. I highly recommend you do the same.

As when I choose my chicken, I only buy locally and humanely raised ducks. I usually get my birds from D'Artagnan. I began buying from them when they first started their farm and company and continue to today.

THIS RECIPE is a perennial favorite in my home. Over the years, I've experimented with many techniques, and this one is easily the best. Brining keeps the meat moist, and brining with konbu adds an amazing savory succulence. To get crackling skin over the juicy meat, I broil the cut pieces just before serving. The combination of textures is out of this world.

crisp savory roast chicken SERVES 4

BRINE

12 sprigs fresh thyme

7 stems fresh basil

2 sprigs fresh rosemary

3 (9 × 6-inch) sheets konbu (see Pantry, page 253)

1 lemon, halved

1 cup kosher salt

1 tablespoon plus 1 teaspoon packed light brown sugar

CHICKEN

1 whole (3-pound) chicken, preferably free-range

1 lemon, halved, plus wedges for serving

1 garlic clove, smashed

8 sprigs fresh thyme

1 sprig fresh rosemary

1 stem fresh basil

Extra-virgin olive oil

Freshly ground black pepper

c'est bon The wire rack you use for cooling cookies can do double duty as a roasting rack. Simply set it inside a rimmed baking sheet. By roasting a chicken—or anything for that matter—on a rack, you get even heat circulation all around and avoid a soggy bottom. Also, raising the food above the rim of the pan helps it brown nicely.

(recipe continues)

To prepare the brine, crush the thyme, basil, and rosemary with your hands and drop into a large, deep bowl or pot. Add the konbu, lemon, salt, sugar, and 1 gallon hot water. Stir until the salt and sugar dissolve. Set inside a large bowl of ice and water (or simply refrigerate) and stir until cool.

Completely submerge the chicken in the brine. Cover tightly and refrigerate for 12 hours.

To roast the chicken, preheat the oven to 350°F. Set a wire rack on a rimmed baking sheet.

Remove the chicken from the brine; discard the brine. Use paper towels to pat the chicken completely dry. Stuff with the lemon, garlic, thyme, rosemary, and basil. Truss the chicken by tying together the legs and securing the wings against the body with kitchen twine. Use a sharp knife to score each leg and thigh with 3 long cuts, each ½ inch deep, to ensure that the dark meat is cooked through before the breast dries out. Rub 1 teaspoon oil all over the chicken and set it on the rack. Place in the oven, cavity side facing front.

Roast for 25 minutes, then rotate the pan and roast for 20 minutes longer. Raise the oven temperature to 375°F and roast for 10 minutes longer or until the juices run clear when you tip the chicken. Remove from the oven and let rest for 15 minutes.

Heat the oven to broil. Arrange the oven rack 6 inches from the heat source.

Cut the chicken into 4 pieces (2 breasts, 2 whole legs). Return to the rack, skin side up. Drizzle with a little oil, then broil until the skin is crackling and crisp, about 2 minutes.

Transfer the chicken to a serving plate and pour the pan juices all over. Sprinkle with pepper and serve with lemon wedges.

BONELESS, SKINLESS chicken breasts are often derided as dry and bland. But I love pounding them and then grilling them until juicy. Their subtlety makes them perfect for a range of flavors—especially in salads. This is one I eat throughout autumn as a complete meal.

grilled chicken salad with apples and roquefort SERVES 4

3 tablespoons chopped fresh
mint leaves

2 tablespoons chopped fresh
tarragon leaves

1 tablespoon chopped fresh
thyme leaves

1 teaspoon finely grated fresh
lemon zest

½ teaspoon freshly ground
black pepper, plus more to
taste

¼ cup extra-virgin olive oil

4 boneless, skinless chicken
breast halves, pounded to an
even ¼-inch thickness

Kosher salt

1 Belgian endive, leaves
separated and sliced

2 cups frisée lettuce, chopped

1⅓ cups baby arugula

1 cup diced radicchio

1 avocado, halved, pitted,
peeled, and diced

1 Gala apple, cored and
julienned

1 cup Candied Paprika Pecans
(page 29)

Red Wine Citrus Vinaigrette
(page 244)

1¾ ounces Roquefort or other
blue cheese, crumbled
(⅓ cup)

c'est bon To get an even ¼-inch-thick chicken breast, you don't simply pound away. Put the chicken breast smooth side down on a work surface. Cut a slit lengthwise straight down the center, stopping ¼ inch from the bottom. At the base of the slit, turn the knife 90 degrees and cut along one side parallel to the bottom of the chicken, but don't cut through the end. Repeat on the other side. Open the two flaps you've just created. Gently pound the chicken until nice and flat.

Heat your grill to high. Use a lightly oiled kitchen towel to carefully grease the grill grate.

In a small bowl, combine the mint, tarragon, thyme, zest, pepper, and oil. Generously season the chicken with salt, then rub the herb oil all over. Grill the chicken, turning once, until just cooked through, about 3 minutes. Transfer to a cutting board and let rest while you make the salad.

In a large bowl, gently toss the endive, frisée, arugula, radicchio, avocado, apple, and pecans with the vinaigrette until well mixed.

Divide the salad among serving plates. Slice the chicken and divide among the salad. Sprinkle the cheese over the chicken. Serve immediately.

fermented soybean paste, is the ultimate marinade. It infuses chicken with a subtle yet intense salty-sweetness. Both leafy and woody herbs add freshness to this summer cookout dish.

miso-marinated grilled chicken

SERVES 4

2 whole (2½-pound) chickens

2 lemons

2 tablespoons white (shiro) miso (see Pantry, page 253)

2 tablespoons finely chopped fresh mint leaves

2 teaspoons finely chopped fresh rosemary leaves

1 fresh red Thai chile, finely chopped

1 garlic clove, minced

2 tablespoons extra-virgin olive oil

Kosher salt and freshly ground black pepper

Lime wedges, for serving

c'est bon Run a sharp knife along the breastbone and wishbone, then down along the side of the rib cage. Continue cutting along the carcass and then along the thighbone. Cut through the edge of the thigh, where it meets the back and the drumstick, to separate the chicken steak from the carcass. Repeat on the other side and with the other chicken. Reserve the chicken legs, wings, and carcasses for another use. (Alternatively, use 1½ pounds boneless chicken breasts and thighs and adjust cooking times accordingly.)

Make boneless chicken steaks, removing the breast and thigh from each side in a single piece without any bones; the two parts will be connected by skin and a little meat (see C'est Bon).

Grate the zest from the lemons into a large, shallow dish. Squeeze ¼ cup juice from the lemons and add to the dish. Add the miso, mint, rosemary, chile, garlic, and oil. Mix well. Add the chicken to the marinade and massage the marinade into the meat. Cover the dish and refrigerate overnight.

Heat your grill to medium. Use a lightly oiled kitchen towel to carefully grease the grill grate.

Rub the chicken in the marinade again. Generously season the chicken with salt and pepper, then place on the grill, skin side down. Cook until the skin is charred, about 5 minutes, then flip. Cook until the meat between the breast and tender is just rosy, about 7 minutes.

Transfer to a serving platter and let rest for 6 minutes. Serve with lime wedges.

EVERY HOME in France has a version of this rustic dish—now my home in New York does as well. I love how the vinegar infuses the chicken with a rich tanginess. Be sure to have some good bread on hand to sop up the sauce.

chicken with vinegar   SERVES 4

1 whole (3-pound) chicken or 2¾ pounds bone-in chicken parts, breasts halved

Kosher salt and freshly ground black pepper

2 tablespoons extra-virgin olive oil

4 tablespoons (½ stick) unsalted butter

4 garlic cloves

3 fresh thyme sprigs

2 dried bay leaves

1½ cups dry white wine

½ cup red wine vinegar

2 medium shallots, diced

4 medium tomatoes, peeled, cored, seeded, and cut into 1-inch pieces (see Note)

1 tablespoon tomato paste

¼ cup chopped fresh herb leaves, preferably a mix of chervil, basil, and flat-leaf parsley

To cut up a whole chicken, start by cutting the wings off through the wing joints, keeping the drumettes on the body. Cut off the wing tips and save for stock. Pull a drumstick away from the body and slice through the skin connecting it to the body, then along the backbone and through the hip joint to remove the thigh. Repeat on the other side. To separate the drumsticks from the thighs, cut through the joint connecting them. Remove the drumette with a portion of the breast: On one thick side of one breast, start cutting about 2 inches above the drumette at a 45-degree angle to the breastbone down through the joint connecting the drumette. Repeat on the other side. Stand the carcass upright, wishbone down. Cut off the breasts—while keeping them on the bone—by cutting through the rib cage. Save the back for stock. Cut the breasts crosswise through the breastbone into 2 even pieces, about the same size as the thighs.

Heat a large Dutch oven or pot over high heat until hot. Generously season the chicken pieces with salt and pepper. Add the oil and 2 tablespoons of the butter to the pot. When the butter melts, add the chicken skin side down, dark-meat pieces first, along with the garlic. Don't crowd the pot; work in batches if necessary. Cook, undisturbed, until the skin is golden brown and releases easily from the pan, about 5 minutes. Flip and cook

(recipe continues)

until the other side is browned, about 2 minutes longer. Transfer to a plate.

Add the thyme, bay leaves, wine, and vinegar to the Dutch oven. Bring the mixture to a boil over high heat. Return all of the chicken to the pot and cover. Reduce the heat to medium-high and cook the breast pieces for 10 minutes or until cooked through. Transfer to a plate. Cook the dark-meat pieces for 7 minutes longer or until the meat pulls away from the bone. Transfer to the same plate.

While the chicken cooks, heat the remaining 2 table-spoons butter in a large skillet over medium-low heat. Just before the butter melts, add the shallots and cook, stirring occasionally, until golden, about 2 minutes. Stir in the tomatoes and tomato paste and season with salt and pepper. Simmer, stirring occasionally, until saucy, about 20 minutes.

After removing the chicken, continue simmering the juices in the Dutch oven until reduced slightly, about 5 minutes. Strain through a fine-mesh sieve into the tomato mixture.

Return the chicken to the Dutch oven in a single layer. Pour the tomato sauce over. Bring to a boil over high heat, then remove from the heat. Add the herbs. Cover and let stand for 20 minutes before serving.

note To peel and seed a tomato, cut a slit in the bottom. Drop the tomato into rapidly boiling water. Heat for 10 seconds or until the skin starts to curl away from the slit. Remove with a slotted spoon and let sit until cool enough to handle. Starting from the slit, peel off the skin. Cut the tomato in half through its equator, then remove the seeds with your fingers.

YOU DON'T NEED bread crumbs in my take on chicken parm. The blend of finely and coarsely grated cheese with just a little flour creates a crunchy, savory crust. I love to serve this with Salsify in Lemon Butter (page 192).

parmesan-crusted chicken SERVES 8

6-ounce block Parmigiano-
  Reggiano cheese
Kosher salt and freshly ground
  black pepper
1 cup all-purpose flour
2 large egg whites
Extra-virgin olive oil
8 (4-ounce) boneless, skinless
  chicken breast halves (each
  ½ inch thick)

Arrange an oven rack in the lowest position. Preheat the oven to 425°F.

Using a box grater, grate half of the cheese on the small holes and the rest on the large holes. Put all the cheese in a shallow dish, along with 1 teaspoon salt and ½ cup of the flour. Toss until evenly mixed. Spread the remaining flour in an even layer in another shallow dish. Whisk the egg whites in a shallow bowl until foamy.

Coat a large rimmed baking sheet with oil to a depth of ⅛ inch. Lightly season the chicken breasts with salt and pepper. Dredge the flat, smooth side of each chicken breast in the plain flour, shake off the excess, then dredge in the egg, and finally press into the Parmesan mixture. Put the chicken, Parmesan side down, in the pan, spacing the breasts apart.

Bake until the crust is golden brown and the meat between the tender and breast is still rosy, about 10 minutes. Remove from the oven, carefully flip the breasts in the pan, and let stand for 2 minutes. Serve immediately.

IF YOU WANT the crunch of fried chicken without the fuss of cooking big pieces, you have to try this quick, streamlined recipe. My technique for cutting chicken steaks gives each person white and dark meat and makes for a hearty serving. This all-season dish is perfect with simply blanched vegetables. In the winter, I serve it with broccoli; in the spring, snap and snow peas; and in the summer, wax beans and haricots verts.

crunchy roasted chicken steaks with mustard sauce SERVES 4

5 tablespoons Dijon mustard
3½ tablespoons fresh lemon
   juice
1 large egg yolk
½ teaspoon Tabasco sauce
Kosher salt and freshly ground
   black pepper
⅔ cup grapeseed or other
   neutral oil, plus more for
   frying

¼ cup extra-virgin olive oil
2 whole (2½-pound) chickens
Cornstarch, as needed
2 tablespoons Herb Butter
   (recipe follows)
Fresh tarragon leaves, for
   garnish

Preheat the oven to 450°F.

Combine the mustard, lemon juice, 2 tablespoons water, the yolk, Tabasco, and 1 teaspoon salt in a blender. Puree until smooth. With the machine running, add both oils in a steady stream and blend to emulsify.

Make boneless chicken steaks, removing the breast and thigh from each side in a single piece without any bones; the two parts will be connected by skin and a little meat (see C'est Bon on page 132).

Generously season the chicken on both sides with salt and pepper. Dust with cornstarch to coat, shaking off excess.

Fill a large skillet with grapeseed oil to a depth of ¼ inch. Heat over high heat until almost smoking. Working in batches, add the chicken, skin side down, and cook until golden, about 2 minutes. Transfer to a baking sheet, skin side up. Repeat with the remaining chicken, then roast in the oven until crunchy and the meat between the tender and breast is just a little rosy, about 11 minutes.

Transfer to a serving platter and top each portion with ½ tablespoon herb butter. Garnish with tarragon. Serve immediately with the mustard sauce.

herb butter MAKES ABOUT ¾ CUP

This simple blend of high-quality butter and fresh fines herbes goes with everything. You can even use it to butter good bread. I especially like it on vegetables and fish.

10 tablespoons unsalted butter,
    preferably cultured, at room
    temperature
Grated zest of 2 lemons
1 tablespoon finely chopped fresh
    tarragon leaves
1 tablespoon finely chopped fresh
    chervil leaves
1 tablespoon finely chopped fresh
    flat-leaf parsley leaves
1 tablespoon minced fresh chives
1 teaspoon Maldon salt or other
    flaky sea salt

In a large bowl, stir together the butter, zest, tarragon, chervil, parsley, chives, and salt until well blended. Transfer to a sheet of plastic wrap and form into a log. Wrap tightly and refrigerate until firm. The butter can be refrigerated for up to 1 week.

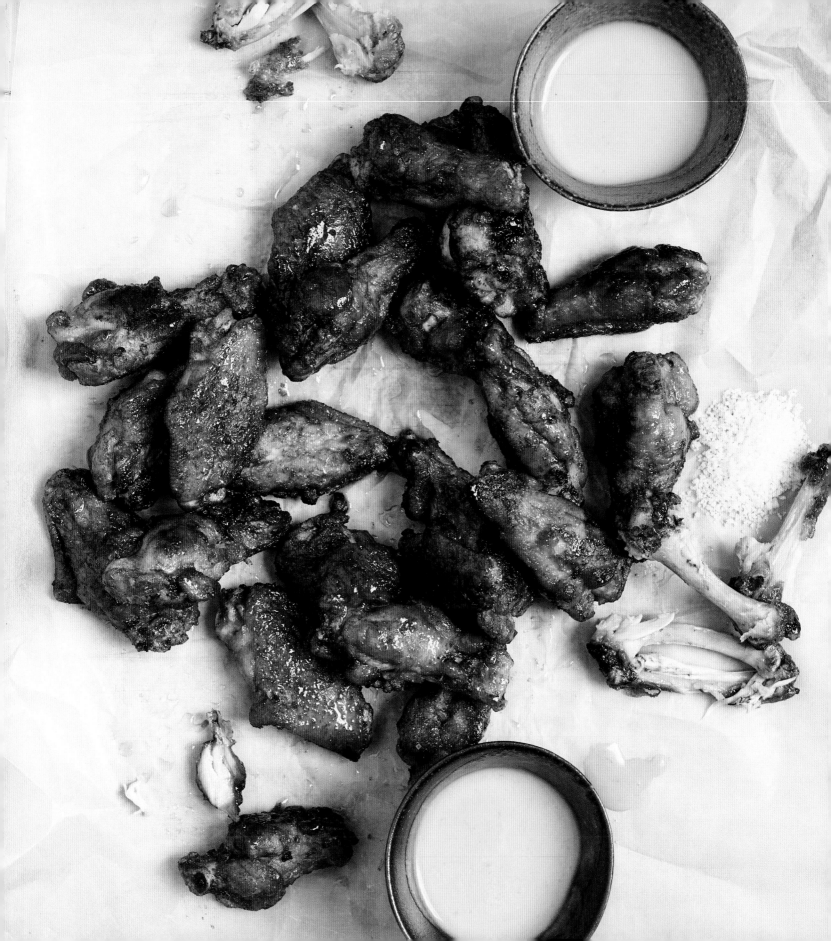

TALK ABOUT addictive. My director of creative development, Greg Brainin, created these, and I can't get enough of them. For a double dose of heat, fresh chile slices cling to the fiery sauce on the crisp wings.

hot wings SERVES 2

2 tablespoons Scotch Bonnet
  Hot Sauce (page 248)
1 tablespoon unsalted butter,
  at room temperature
Kosher salt and freshly ground
  black pepper
6 whole chicken wings, wings
  and drumettes separated,
  wing tips removed
1 tablespoon cornstarch
Grapeseed or other neutral oil
½ jalapeño, very thinly sliced
  crosswise

In a small saucepan, heat the sauce over medium heat until hot. Whisk in the butter, a little at a time. Continue whisking until the mixture is emulsified. Whisk in salt to taste, then reduce the heat to low to keep the sauce warm.

Sprinkle salt and pepper all over the chicken and let stand for 5 minutes to release the moisture on the skin. Sprinkle the cornstarch all over the chicken and toss until evenly coated.

Fill a large skillet with oil to a depth of ½ inch. Heat over high heat until hot and shimmering. (When the oil is ready, a cube of bread dropped into it will turn golden in 15 seconds.)

Reduce the heat to medium and add the drumettes first, then the wings in a single layer. Cook, turning the chicken with tongs, for 4 minutes. Raise the heat to high. Cook, turning occasionally, until the chicken is golden brown outside and no longer pink inside, about 4 minutes longer.

Transfer the chicken to a large bowl and add the hot sauce and jalapeño. Toss until evenly coated. Serve immediately.

MY ALSATIAN upbringing and my time in Asia often merge in my cooking. This take on classic Cantonese roasted duck pairs beautifully with Sweet and Sour Cabbage (page 193). I love when the soy-infused duck juices run into the tender vegetables.

soy-syrup roasted duck   SERVES 4

Grapeseed or other neutral oil
1 whole (4½-pound) Muscovy
   duck, excess fat removed,
   trussed
Kosher salt and freshly ground
   black pepper
½ cup grade A maple syrup
½ cup unseasoned rice vinegar
½ cup soy sauce

Preheat the oven to 450°F.

Lightly coat the bottom of a heavy roasting pan with oil. Season the duck generously with salt and pepper and place in the pan, breast side up. Roast for 10 minutes, then carefully turn the duck back side up. Roast for another 10 minutes and then carefully turn on one side. To get the duck to sit upright on a leg, rest the back of the duck against the side of the pan. Roast for another 10 minutes, then carefully turn onto the other side and roast for 10 minutes.

Meanwhile, stir together the maple syrup, vinegar, and soy sauce.

Transfer the duck to a dish and drain the fat through a fine-mesh sieve into a measuring cup. Reserve for another use. Reduce the oven temperature to 375°F.

Return the duck to the roasting pan breast side up. Pour the syrup mixture over, letting it run down the sides. Return to the oven. Roast, basting every 5 minutes, for 20 minutes. Tilt the duck to let its juices run out of the cavity; the juices should be pale pink. Cook for another 5 minutes if needed. Remove from the oven and let rest for 10 minutes, basting frequently.

To carve, first remove the legs by slicing between the legs and body, then through the hip joint. Cut through the leg joint to separate the drumstick from the thigh. Cut the thigh in slices parallel to the thighbone. Pull the wings away from the body, then slice through the wing joints to remove. Run your knife down the breastbone, then along the rib cage to remove a breast. Repeat on the other side. Cut the breasts crosswise into slices.

Arrange the sliced duck on a serving platter. Spoon the glaze from the pan all over.

c'est bon Before trussing the duck, cut 2 slits along the wishbone. That will make it easy to remove the bone after the duck has cooked. It's much easier to carve a duck without it.

IF YOU WANT to impress at a dinner party, this is the dish to make. The secret ingredient? Jordan almonds, those impossibly hard candies handed out at weddings. They turn into a gorgeous caramelized crust on the roasted duck breast. Simply cooked baby turnips make an elegant accompaniment.

almond-caramelized duck breasts with amaretto jus SERVES 4

½ cup red wine vinegar

⅓ cup amaretto

⅓ cup ruby port

⅓ cup dry red wine

¾ teaspoon fennel seeds

4 (6-ounce) boneless, skin-on duck breast halves

Kosher salt and freshly ground black pepper

1 teaspoon grapeseed or other neutral oil

1 cup Jordan almonds, preferably all white

2 teaspoons honey

3 tablespoons unsalted butter, at room temperature

Arrange one oven rack in the lowest position. Place another oven rack 8 inches from the broiler heat source. Preheat the oven to 450°F.

Bring the vinegar, amaretto, port, wine, and fennel to a boil over high heat in a medium saucepan. Continue boiling rapidly until syrupy and reduced to ⅓ cup, about 20 minutes.

Meanwhile, heat a large ovenproof skillet over high heat. Season both sides of the duck breasts with salt and pepper. Add the oil to the pan, swirling to coat the bottom, then add the duck, skin side down. Transfer the pan to the lowest rack in the oven. Cook until the skin is dark golden brown and the meat feels firm, 10 to 12 minutes.

Transfer the duck to a rimmed baking sheet, skin side up. Let rest for 5 minutes. (The meat will be medium-rare.) Heat the oven to broil, preferably a low broil setting if you have it.

With another heavy skillet, firmly press down on the almonds until they are all crushed into tiny bits. Spread the crushed almonds in a thin, even layer. Spoon ½ teaspoon honey on the skin side of each duck breast, then press into the almonds. Return to the baking sheet, skin

side up. Fill in any gaps with the almonds; the whole skin side should be evenly coated.

Broil until the almonds are toasted and the sugar starts to melt, about 7 minutes. Check on the crust occasionally; you don't want the almonds to burn before the sugar starts to melt. Remove from the broiler and let rest for 5 minutes.

While the duck rests, heat the sauce over low heat until hot. Whisk in the butter, a little at a time, until the sauce emulsifies. Season the sauce with salt and pepper to taste. Divide the sauce among serving plates and arrange a duck breast on each.

DANIEL DEL VECCHIO has been working with me for nearly twenty years. For a long time, he was known as my right-hand man—and for good reason. That's why I now entrust him with opening and maintaining my restaurants around the world. More important, he's like family. We've celebrated many holidays and milestones together, including, of course, Thanksgiving, when his turkey has often been the star of the show.

dan's thanksgiving turkey SERVES 12 TO 14

4 cups kosher salt, plus more as needed

¾ cup sugar

1 whole (12- to 14-pound) turkey, giblets and neck reserved

4 medium yellow onions, chopped

4 carrots, chopped

4 celery stalks, chopped

½ bunch fresh flat-leaf parsley

12 fresh thyme sprigs

6 tablespoons (¾ stick) unsalted butter, at room temperature

1 head garlic, cloves separated and crushed

12 whole chicken wings

1 tablespoon cornstarch

Soy sauce

Freshly ground black pepper

In a large stockpot, stir together the salt, sugar, and 2 gallons water until the salt and sugar dissolve. Submerge the turkey in the brine and refrigerate for 4 to 6 hours.

Remove the turkey from the brine, rinse, and pat dry. Refrigerate, uncovered, for 8 to 24 hours.

Arrange an oven rack in the lowest position. Preheat the oven to 400°F.

Put the turkey, breast side down, in the center of a large, heavy roasting pan. Stuff with a third of the onions, carrots, celery, parsley, thyme, and 1 tablespoon of the butter. Truss well.

Scatter the garlic, chicken wings, turkey giblets and neck, and the remaining vegetables and herbs around the bird. Pour 1 cup water over the vegetables. Melt the remaining 5 tablespoons butter and brush all over the turkey.

Roast for 45 minutes. Turn the turkey so that one wing side is up and baste, adding water to the pan if it is dry. Roast for 15 minutes longer, then turn the turkey so that the other wing side is up. Baste, then roast for 15 minutes longer. Turn the turkey breast side up, baste, and roast until the internal temperature of the leg registers 170°F, 30 to 40 minutes longer. Remove from the oven, tent with foil, and let rest for 20 to 30 minutes.

While the turkey rests, remove the turkey neck and giblets from the pan. Pick the meat from the neck and dice. Dice the giblets.

Tilt the turkey to pour its juices into the roasting pan, then transfer the turkey to a serving platter. Set a fine-mesh sieve over a measuring cup. Carefully pour all the liquid from the pan through the sieve; discard the solids. Let stand for a few minutes, then spoon off the fat from the juices, discarding the fat, or use a fat separator. Pour the pan juices back into the roasting pan. Add the neck meat and giblets to the pan. Straddle the pan between 2 burners and bring the juices to a boil. Stir 1 tablespoon water into the cornstarch, then stir into the juices. Boil until thickened slightly, about 2 minutes. Season to taste with soy sauce, salt, and pepper and then transfer to a gravy boat.

Carve the turkey and serve with the gravy.

meat

MY SON, CEDRIC, THE CHEF DE cuisine at my restaurant Perry Street, is a great chef. When he was younger, I actually tried to dissuade him from joining this grueling profession, but I'm glad I didn't convince him. He turns out amazing food at the restaurant as well as in our home. On the weekends, he's our meat cook. And my brother Philippe builds hot fires with lump wood charcoal for grilling.

As with everything else, sourcing the best ingredients is key. It's so much harder to do that now than when I was growing up in France. There, all of our beef was grass-fed and raised naturally and slowly without growth hormones or antibiotics. I love the complex flavor and texture of grass-fed beef. I get my beef from DeBragga and suggest you go online to find local purveyors of sustainably raised meat.

But as much as I love a good steak, I'm really more of a pork guy. In my childhood home, we kept a pork box in the fridge. It was always stocked with ham, bacon, chops, sausages, head cheese. Nowadays, I get my Berkshire pork from Flying Pigs Farm. For choucroute and other Alsatian specialties, I go to Schaller & Weber. When I'm craving lamb or veal instead, I buy from Mosner Family Brands.

A few meat pointers: Be sure to thoroughly dry meat with paper towels before you begin. Season it with salt just before cooking—not earlier—to prevent any moisture from forming on the surface. And let cooked meat rest before slicing.

MY WIFE, Marja, makes the best truly authentic Korean bulgogi. This is my take on that dish, with a hint of orange and a little heat. Instead of starting with thinly sliced meat, as is traditional, I cook a whole flank steak and then slice it just before serving.

bulgogi-marinated grilled flank steak SERVES 2 TO 4

Grated zest of ½ orange

1 garlic clove, minced to a paste

1 scallion, white and green parts, minced

2 tablespoons soy sauce

1 teaspoon packed dark brown sugar

½ teaspoon sriracha (see Pantry, page 253)

½ teaspoon sesame oil

¼ teaspoon crushed red chile flakes

1 whole (1-pound) flank steak

Kosher salt and freshly ground black pepper

In a shallow dish large enough to hold the steak, combine the zest, garlic, scallion, soy sauce, sugar, sriracha, sesame oil, and chile flakes. Use a fork to poke holes all over the steak. Add the steak to the marinade and massage the marinade into the meat. Cover the dish and refrigerate for 12 hours.

Heat your grill to high. Use a lightly oiled kitchen towel to carefully grease the grill grate. Let the steak stand at room temperature for 10 minutes while the grill heats.

Rub the steak in the marinade again; it should all be absorbed. Generously season the steak with salt and pepper, then place on the grill. Cook until the bottom releases easily from the grill, about 2 minutes, then flip and cook, flipping every 45 seconds, to desired doneness, about 6 minutes longer for medium-rare.

Transfer to a cutting board and let rest for 5 minutes. Slice against the grain at an angle and serve.

c'est bon If you don't have a lot of time to marinate, cut the steak in quarters first to increase the surface area exposed to the marinade. Reduce the cooking time accordingly—a minute or two less.

AFTER MY BROTHER Philippe builds the perfect fire in the grill, my son, Cedric, cooks the perfect whole tenderloin. Quickly marinating the beef in herbs and oil and then using that oil to baste the beef keeps the lean meat from drying out and infuses it with flavor. Serve this with good mustard or Barbecue Sauce (page 247).

cedric's grilled beef tenderloin SERVES 12

1 whole (5- to 6-pound) beef
   tenderloin, trimmed
1 garlic clove, halved
Extra-virgin olive oil
10 sprigs fresh thyme, torn
   into small pieces
2 sprigs fresh rosemary, torn
   into small pieces
Kosher salt and freshly ground
   black pepper

c'est bon If you're buying beef tenderloin already trimmed, look for a 4½- to 5-pound one. If you want to trim one yourself, start by pulling off the excess fat all over the beef. Gently pull the chain away from the main tenderloin. The long, thin chain muscle runs almost the entire length of the tenderloin. With a very sharp knife, cut off the chain. Then cut off the head (sometimes referred to as the butt) of the tenderloin. This is the large muscle on one end. Reserve for another use or grill separately to well done for those who prefer the meat fully cooked. Remove the silverskin by sliding your knife just under it 1 inch from the end. Cut through the end, then turn your knife around and slice off a ½-inch strip of the silverskin, using a very slow sawing motion. Don't pull the silverskin while you're cutting; just lift it and run your knife along it, a ½-inch strip at a time.

Heat your grill to medium-high. Use a lightly oiled kitchen towel to carefully grease the grill grate.

Put the tenderloin on a rimmed baking sheet or platter. Rub the cut sides of the garlic all over the meat. Generously brush oil all over the beef to coat completely. Pat the thyme and rosemary into the beef. Let stand for 7 minutes. Turn the beef over and rub any fallen herbs on top. Let stand for 7 minutes longer.

Use your hand to brush off the herbs and excess oil from the beef, reserving the herb oil. You want just a very thin sheen of oil and bits of thyme and rosemary leaves on the beef. Generously season the beef with salt and pepper, then place on the hot grill. Grill until the bottom is crusty and caramelized, about 7 minutes. Flip the beef over and brush the browned side with some of the reserved herb oil. Grill for 7 minutes longer, then flip onto one side, brushing the browned sides with some herb oil. Grill for 7 minutes longer, then repeat with the last side, grilling for 7 minutes longer for medium rare. A cake tester or thin-bladed knife inserted in the center of the beef for a few seconds should feel warm when you press it under your lips.

Transfer to a cutting board and brush with fresh oil until nice and shiny. Let rest for at least 15 minutes. Slice and serve immediately.

THIS DISH IS unbelievable. It may just be one of my favorite ways to eat steak. The complex depth of floral, almost fruity flavors in this hot sauce shines when served with a simply grilled steak and cuts through the richness of the meat.

seared steaks with buttery hot sauce   SERVES 2 TO 4

2 (10-ounce) dry-aged strip
   loin steaks (each 1½ inches
   thick)
⅔ cup Scotch Bonnet Hot
   Sauce (page 248)
7 tablespoons unsalted butter,
   at room temperature
Kosher salt and freshly ground
   black pepper
Grapeseed or other neutral oil

Arrange one oven rack in the lowest position. Preheat the oven to 400°F. Let the steaks stand at room temperature for 10 minutes while the oven heats and pat them very dry with paper towels.

In a small saucepan, heat the sauce over medium heat until hot. Whisk in 6 tablespoons of the butter, a little at a time. Continue whisking until the mixture is emulsified. Whisk in 1 teaspoon salt, then reduce the heat to low and keep the sauce warm.

Heat a large cast-iron or other ovenproof skillet over high heat until hot. Coat the bottom of the hot pan with oil. Season both sides of the steaks generously with salt and pepper. When the oil is almost smoking, add the steaks. Sear for 1 minute, then use tongs to pick up each steak and put it back down on the same side. Cook for 1 minute longer, then flip the steaks and transfer the skillet to the oven.

Roast for 4 minutes, then add the remaining 1 table-spoon butter to the skillet. Baste the steak with the melted butter and pan juices and roast for 1 minute longer for medium-rare. Baste again, then transfer to a cutting board and let rest for 5 minutes.

Slice the steaks, transfer to a serving platter with their juices, and spoon the hot sauce all over.

THE DRESSING and pickles here are magic—they make the burger. Sometimes, I make full-size burgers with 7-ounce patties, but I generally prefer sliders. That way, you can eat more of everything else you serve on the side. The best burger meat comes from aged beef chuck that is freshly ground by your butcher.

sliders with russian dressing and yuzu pickles SERVES 12

2¾ pounds freshly ground beef chuck, preferably aged
Kosher salt and freshly ground black pepper
12 slices pepper Jack cheese
12 mini kaiser or brioche rolls, split
Russian Dressing (page 246)
12 small Boston lettuce leaves
Yuzu Pickles (page 249)
24 tomato slices, from about 6 smaller tomatoes

Heat your grill to medium-high. Use a lightly oiled kitchen towel to carefully grease the grill grate.

Form the beef into 12 patties 3 inches in diameter and 1 inch high. Generously season with salt and pepper. Grill for 2 to 4 minutes per side for medium-rare. During the last minute of grilling, top each burger with a slice of cheese.

Grill the cut sides of the rolls alongside the patties until golden brown and crisp, 1 to 2 minutes. Transfer to a serving plate.

Spread a generous layer of dressing on both sides of each roll. Arrange the lettuce on the bottom of each roll, cupped sides up (to capture the mouthwatering meat juices). Transfer the patties to the lettuce-lined buns and immediately top each with a thin layer of tomatoes and then pickles. Season the tomatoes with a little salt. Cover with the buns' tops and serve immediately.

CHERRIES AND MUSTARD may sound like an unusual pairing, but they taste great together. Sweet, tart, and hot, this sauce goes well with chicken and veal as well as pork.

pork chops with cherry mustard SERVES 4

2 tablespoons Colman's dry mustard

1 teaspoon kosher salt

1 pound Bing cherries, stemmed and pitted (3 cups packed)

½ cup red wine vinegar

¼ cup ruby port

2 tablespoons sugar

2 tablespoons cumin seeds, finely ground

3 tablespoons sherry vinegar

¼ cup honey

4 (9-ounce) bone-in pork chops, preferably Berkshire (each 1¼ inches thick)

In a medium bowl, stir together the mustard and 1 tablespoon water until smooth. Let stand for 15 minutes. Stir in the salt until well combined.

Meanwhile, in a medium saucepan, boil the cherries, red wine vinegar, port, and sugar over high heat, stirring occasionally, until syrupy, about 10 minutes. Transfer to a blender and puree until smooth.

Return the mixture to the saucepan and bring to a boil over high heat. Boil, stirring occasionally, until the consistency of ketchup, about 5 minutes. Stir the cherry mixture into the mustard mixture, a little at a time, until completely incorporated. This mustard will keep in the refrigerator for up to 3 days.

Heat your grill to medium-high. Use a lightly oiled kitchen towel to carefully grease the grill grate.

In a small bowl, stir together the cumin, sherry vinegar, and honey. Reserve 1 tablespoon in another bowl and use the rest to brush all over the pork. Let the pork stand for 5 minutes while the grill heats.

Grill the pork, turning every 45 seconds to cook evenly, until the center is still a little pink, about 8 minutes. Remove from the grill, brush with the reserved honey mixture, and let rest for 10 minutes. Serve with the cherry mustard.

c'est bon Whenever I'm adding a very hot mixture to a room temperature one, as with the cherry and mustard here, I add just a tiny bit at first and gradually add more and more. It's important to temper it; otherwise, you'll end up with globs of mustard paste in your sauce.

TRUE, FAVA BEANS are a pain. First, you have to shell the beans, then peel off their tissue-thin skins. To be honest, though, I actually enjoy prepping these beans—especially if it means getting to eat them. Simply cooked, they're the perfect accompaniment to juicy lamb chops.

lamb chops with smoked chile glaze and warm fava beans   SERVES 4

8 double-rib lamb chops
  (about 2 pounds total),
  frenched
Kosher salt and freshly ground
  black pepper
2 pounds fava bean pods,
  shelled (3 cups beans)
Smoked Chile Glaze (page 247)
2 tablespoons extra-virgin
  olive oil

Heat your grill to medium. Use a lightly oiled kitchen towel to carefully grease the grill grate. Let the lamb chops stand at room temperature for 5 minutes while the grill heats.

Bring a large saucepan of water to a boil over high heat and salt it. Fill a large bowl with ice and water. Add the fava beans to the boiling water and cook just until the water returns to a full boil, about 2 minutes. Drain the favas and immediately transfer to the ice water. When cool, drain again, then peel the thin skins off the beans.

Pour ¼ cup of the chile glaze into a small dish. Season the lamb chops with salt and pepper, then brush both sides of each chop with a thin layer of the ¼ cup glaze. Grill, covered, for 15 minutes for medium-rare, turning and brushing with a thin layer of glaze every 5 minutes. Transfer to serving plates and let rest while preparing the favas.

Combine the peeled fava beans, the oil, and 2 tablespoons water in a medium saucepan over medium heat. Cook, stirring, until warm, about 2 minutes.

Divide the favas among the serving plates and serve with the remaining glaze on the side.

AS QUICK AS a stir-fry, this is my go-to fast food. My take on veal scaloppine uses ham, Riesling, and, best of all, lavender. The floral herb is similar to sage and works beautifully here. I prefer the aroma of the tiny purple buds on the flowers, but if you can't find those, the leaves work well, too.

veal scaloppine with broccoli rabe and lavender   SERVES 4

Kosher salt

12 ounces broccoli rabe, trimmed

4 very thin slices traditionally smoked ham

4 (4-ounce) pieces veal scaloppine (¼-inch-thick cutlets)

Freshly ground black pepper

All-purpose flour

Grapeseed oil

1½ cups dry Riesling

6 tablespoons (¾ stick) unsalted butter, at room temperature

¼ teaspoon picked lavender flowers or finely chopped leaves

Bring a large pot of water to a boil. Fill a large bowl with ice and water. Generously season the boiling water with salt and add the broccoli rabe. Cook until just tender, about 5 minutes. Drain and immediately transfer to the ice water. When room temperature, drain again and pat dry with paper towels. Cut into 3-inch lengths.

Place 1 slice of ham on top of each veal cutlet. Slip between sheets of plastic wrap. Use a meat mallet to gently pound the ham into the veal. Lightly season with salt and pepper, then dredge in flour until completely coated.

Fill a large skillet with oil to a depth of ¼ inch. Heat over high heat until very hot; it should shimmer. Shake excess flour off a scaloppine and slide into the pan, ham side down. Cook until golden brown and crisp, about 2 minutes. Carefully flip and cook for 5 seconds more. Drain on paper towels. Repeat with the remaining scaloppine, replenishing and reheating oil between batches as needed.

Drain all of the oil from the skillet. Add the Riesling and butter and cook, stirring, over high heat until emulsified, golden, and reduced to the consistency of a glaze, about 3 minutes. Season lightly with salt.

Add the broccoli rabe to the sauce and cook, tossing gently, until well coated and warm.

Arrange the veal, ham side up, on serving dishes and top with the broccoli rabe and sauce. Season with pepper and sprinkle the lavender flowers over the top.

I LOVE MEATY short ribs, but I don't want the fuss of browning the ribs before braising them at home. To get that same rich, caramelized flavor, I simply cook the beef with konbu. Notable for its umami, this one ingredient can deliver the same depth of flavor that comes from searing meat. I do labor over these ribs, though; at the end, I keep glazing them until they shine. Serve with Honey-Glazed Parsnips (page 201) for an inspired combination.

glazed short ribs SERVES 8

3 cups dry red wine

7½ pounds bone-in short ribs, separated into whole ribs

Kosher salt

2 whole heads garlic, cut in half through their equators

5 large fresh shiitake mushroom caps, halved

2 carrots, peeled and chopped

2 medium yellow onions, peeled and quartered

1 small celery stalk, chopped

4-inch piece fresh ginger, peeled and sliced

11 whole allspice berries, lightly crushed

1 cinnamon stick

1 (6 × 5-inch) sheet konbu (see Pantry, page 253)

½ small bunch fresh thyme (¼ ounce)

10½ cups chicken stock, preferably homemade

6 tablespoons red wine vinegar

Preheat the oven to 325°F.

Bring the wine to a boil in a large saucepan over high heat. Boil rapidly until reduced to ½ cup.

Generously season the ribs on all sides with salt. Let stand for 10 minutes.

Transfer the ribs to a large roasting pan, bone side up. Scatter the garlic, shiitakes, carrots, onions, celery, ginger, allspice, cinnamon, konbu, and thyme on top of the ribs. Add the stock, vinegar, and reduced red wine. Cover the pan tightly with foil, crimping the edges around the rim of the pan. Transfer to the oven and braise until completely fork-tender, 3½ to 4 hours.

Remove the ribs from the oven and carefully remove the foil. Raise the oven temperature to 375°F.

When cool enough to handle, carefully transfer the ribs to a dish. Remove and discard the bones and any bits of vegetables or herbs clinging to the meat. Set a fine-mesh sieve over a large measuring cup. Carefully pour all the liquid from the pan through the sieve; discard the solids. Let stand for a few minutes, then spoon the fat from the juices, discarding the fat, or use a fat separator. Pour the juices back into the roasting pan.

Return the ribs to the pan in a single layer and straddle the pan between 2 burners. Bring the liquid to a boil, then transfer the pan to the oven. Cook, basting frequently, until the ribs are glazed with a shiny coat, 5 to 10 minutes. The glaze should be saucy and cling to the ribs, but not sticky. And you should have at least 2 cups of it remaining for serving.

Serve the short ribs topped with the glaze.

I THOUGHT I was tired of braised lamb shanks, having cooked them for so many years. But then I added a step that utterly transforms them. Reducing the braising liquid and then basting the lamb with it makes this dish wonderfully rich. Serve this with Green Apple and Jalapeño Duo (page 177); the green apple puree and salad balance the richness with a bright, refreshing acidity.

soy-braised lamb shanks   SERVES 4

Grapeseed or other neutral oil

4 whole (2-pound) lamb shanks, trimmed and patted dry

2 medium yellow onions, sliced

2 medium shallots, sliced

13 garlic cloves, sliced

Kosher salt

2 Asian pears, cored and cut into 2-inch chunks

1 bunch scallions, green parts only

2 lemongrass stalks, smashed and thinly sliced

5-inch piece fresh ginger, peeled and chopped

1 fresh long red (finger) chile, stemmed, seeded, and sliced

4 whole star anise

1¼ cups semidry Gewürztraminer or Riesling

1 cup champagne vinegar

¾ cup soy sauce

½ cup honey

Preheat the oven to 325°F.

Heat a large Dutch oven over high heat until very hot. Add enough oil to generously coat the bottom of the pan and heat until almost smoking. Carefully slide in the lamb shanks in a single layer. Do not crowd the pan; cook in batches if necessary. Cook until golden brown on one side, about 4 minutes. Turn on another side and continue cooking and turning to evenly brown all sides and the top, about 8 minutes longer. Drain all of the fat from the pan.

Meanwhile, heat a large sauté pan over medium heat. Add enough oil to generously coat the bottom of the pan and heat until shimmering. Stir in the onions, shallots, and garlic. Season with a pinch of salt. Cover and cook, stirring occasionally, until golden brown and tender, about 10 minutes.

Add the onion mixture to the pan with the lamb, along with the pears, scallions, lemongrass, ginger,

chile, anise, wine, vinegar, soy sauce, and honey. Add enough water to cover the lamb by ½ inch.

Cover and bring to a boil. Transfer to the oven and braise until the meat is completely tender and falling off the bone, about 3½ hours. Uncover and carefully transfer the lamb shanks to a dish. Raise the oven temperature to 375°F.

Strain the braising liquid through a fine-mesh sieve into a large saucepan, pressing on the solids to extract as much liquid as possible. Bring to a boil and continue to boil over high heat until reduced by a third.

Return the shanks to the Dutch oven, meat side down, and pour the reduced liquid over them. Transfer to the oven and cook, basting every 5 minutes, until lacquered with a mahogany glaze, about 15 minutes. There should still be syrupy sauce left in the pan.

Serve the lamb shanks with the sauce spooned over the meat.

ENJOY THIS ALSATIAN specialty with some good beer. I like making this with crunchy, bright, and tart fresh sauerkraut, which my mom brings me from France. It's also delicious with regular sauerkraut. I love how the meat juices infuse the cabbage and potatoes for a satisfying one-pot meal.

choucroute   SERVES 12

3 tablespoons rendered duck or goose fat or unsalted butter

3 tablespoons unsalted butter

1 large yellow onion, thinly sliced

4 pounds fresh sauerkraut

4 fresh bay leaves

20 juniper berries packed in vinegar, rinsed well, or 1 tablespoon dried juniper berries

Kosher salt

3 fresh pig knuckles

1 rack (about 2 pounds) baby back ribs, cut in half

½ slab fresh bacon (about 4 inches)

½ slab double-smoked bacon (about 4 inches)

4 garlic cloves, very thinly sliced

1 bottle (750 ml) dry Riesling

12 Yukon Gold potatoes, peeled and quartered

5 Alsatian knacks with natural casings or other German frankfurters

Very good Dijon mustard and horseradish sauce, for serving

Heat a 5-quart Dutch oven or pot over medium-low heat. Melt the duck fat and butter, then add the onion. Cook, stirring occasionally, until the onion is softened and golden but not browned, about 10 minutes.

Meanwhile, rinse the sauerkraut under hot water to remove excess salt. When it starts to stick to your fingers, drain well and squeeze out as much liquid as possible with your hands.

Add the sauerkraut, bay leaves, and juniper berries to the onions, season with salt, and stir once. Arrange the knuckles, ribs, and both bacons in the sauerkraut, partially burying them in the mixture. Top with the garlic, then add the wine. Cover, bring to a boil, then reduce the heat and simmer for 2 hours.

About 30 minutes before serving, arrange the potatoes in a single layer over the meat. Cover and continue cooking until the potatoes and meat are tender.

About 20 minutes before serving, place the knacks in a medium saucepan and cover with cold water. Bring to a very gentle simmer and cook until heated through, about 15 minutes. Do not let the water boil or the knacks will explode.

Transfer the potatoes and meat from the Dutch oven to a large serving platter, let cool slightly, and slice the meat. Transfer the sauerkraut to the platter. Top with the knacks. Serve with mustard and horseradish sauce on the side.

side dishes

ON THE WEEKENDS, I VOLUNTEER for side-dish duty. I love cooking and eating everything, but fresh vegetables are simply my favorite. Every weekend, I shop at local farmers' markets and catch up with the farmers, some of whom I've worked with for decades. They teach me so much about the beautiful ingredients they grow.

Just this year, I learned that parsnips are best in late winter and early spring. I had always thought of them as a fall vegetable, but one of my favorite farmers taught me that the roots grow sweeter in the cold months. If they're harvested and kept out, their germs begin to sprout. But if they're harvested and then reburied at least two feet deep in the ground, they keep well. That's what he does with his root vegetables. When they're harvested again, they're mature and super-sweet.

If you're in New York, you can try some of my regular stops at the Greenmarket: Berried Treasures for berries and peas; Cherry Lane Farm for zucchini, corn, and berries; Eckerton Hill Farm for tomatoes; Fantasy Fruit for berries; Locust Grove Fruit Farm for berries, peaches, apricots, and cherries; Migliorelli Farm for Japanese turnips, greens, and plums; Mountain Sweet Berry Farm for Tri-Star strawberries and potatoes; Paffenroth Gardens for greens and root vegetables; Stokes Farm for cherries, garlic, and herbs; and Sycamore Farms for snap peas, broccoli, and zucchini.

green apple and jalapeño duo SERVES 8

PUREE

6 Granny Smith apples
½ lemon
6 tablespoons (¾ stick) unsalted butter
1 small jalapeño, chopped
1 tablespoon kosher salt, plus more to taste

SALAD

2 Granny Smith apples, quartered, cored, and very thinly sliced crosswise
2 celery stalks, very thinly sliced at an angle
2 scallions, very thinly sliced at an angle
1 small jalapeño, very thinly sliced into rings
2 limes
Extra-virgin olive oil
Kosher salt and freshly ground black pepper

To make the puree, peel the apples and put the peels in a bowl. Squeeze lemon juice over them, tossing to coat evenly.

Core the apples and cut into 1-inch pieces. Transfer to a large saucepan, along with the butter, jalapeño, and salt. Cover and cook over medium heat, stirring occasionally, until the apples are just beginning to soften but are still firm in the centers, about 9 minutes.

Transfer to a blender, along with the reserved peels. Puree until very smooth, scraping down the sides of the bowl occasionally. Season with more salt to taste. Serve warm.

To make the salad, combine the apples, celery, scallions, and jalapeño in a large bowl. Cut the limes in wedges and squeeze the juice all over, drizzle with oil, and season with salt and pepper. Toss until evenly dressed. Serve immediately.

THIS SIMPLE almond-shallot topping goes with just about any simply cooked vegetable, but it tastes best with green beans. Instead of simply blanching the beans, I char them until they develop a smoky richness.

pan-roasted green beans with golden almonds SERVES 4

Kosher salt

8 ounces green and/or wax beans, trimmed

¼ cup blanched whole almonds, coarsely chopped

3 tablespoons extra-virgin olive oil, plus more as needed

1 large shallot, minced

1 tablespoon fresh flat-leaf parsley leaves, thinly sliced

1 lemon

Freshly ground black pepper

Bring a large pot of water to a rolling boil and salt it. Fill a large bowl with ice and water. Add the green beans to the boiling water and cook until bright green but still firm, about 2 minutes. Drain and transfer to the ice water. When cool, drain again. Pat dry with paper towels until completely dry.

Meanwhile, in a small saucepan, combine the almonds and the oil, adding more oil if needed to just cover the almonds. Cook over medium heat until the almonds are golden, about 6 minutes. Remove from the heat and stir in the shallot. It will cook in the residual heat.

Coat a large skillet with oil. Heat over medium-high heat until very hot but not smoking. Add the beans and season with salt. Cook, tossing frequently, until charred dark brown in spots and tender-crisp, about 7 minutes.

Top with the almond mixture, then the parsley. Grate the zest from a quarter of the lemon directly over, then cut the lemon into wedges for serving. Season with pepper and serve.

IN SPRING, garden peas and young carrots need little embellishment to taste amazing. It's all about the execution. You want them just tender, but not crunchy. And you use only a little butter here—just enough to make the vegetables glisten.

glazed fresh peas and carrots with mint and dill   SERVES 4

2 thin carrots
1 cup thinly sliced Vidalia
 onion
1½ tablespoons unsalted butter
Kosher salt
2 cups fresh shelled green peas
 (from 2 to 2½ pounds in
 the pod)
2 tablespoons thinly sliced
 fresh mint leaves
1 tablespoon fresh dill leaves

Cut a ½-inch piece from a carrot at an angle. Roll the carrot until the cut side faces up and cut another ½-inch piece at an angle. Continue rolling and cutting both carrots.

Combine the carrots, onion, 1 tablespoon of the butter, ½ teaspoon salt, and 3 tablespoons water in a medium saucepan. Cover and cook over medium heat until very tender, about 10 minutes. A knife should be able to pierce through a carrot with no resistance.

Meanwhile, combine the peas and 3 tablespoons water in a large saucepan. There should be just enough water to coat the bottom of the pan. If there isn't, add more water as needed. Bring to a boil, then simmer, stirring occasionally, over medium heat until the peas are just tender, 8 to 10 minutes.

Add the carrot mixture and the remaining ½ table-spoon butter to the peas. Cook, stirring frequently, until the vegetables are glazed and bound by a thin, creamy sauce, about 2 minutes.

Transfer to a serving bowl and top with mint and dill.

PEOPLE OFTEN ask me why the asparagus in my eponymous restaurant tastes so much better than similar-looking spears they've had elsewhere. The answer is simple: We cook each batch to order. Most kitchens blanch the asparagus early in the day and then reheat it just before serving; a lot of flavor is lost that way. This is one of the first lessons my chef de cuisine Mark Lapico teaches new cooks at my flagship. Once you try this recipe at home, you'll never throw your asparagus in ice water again. Of course, you *can* make this dish with olive oil, but it's especially good with butter.

buttered asparagus with lemon and parmesan SERVES 4

Kosher salt

2 pounds jumbo asparagus (about 16 spears), trimmed and peeled

½ tablespoon unsalted butter

1-ounce block Parmigiano-Reggiano cheese

1 lemon

Freshly ground black pepper

Bring a large pot of water to a rolling boil and salt it. Add the asparagus and cook until bright green and just tender, about 8 minutes. Drain well and transfer to a serving plate.

Rub the butter all over the asparagus until melted. Using a Microplane or other fine grater, grate enough cheese to cover the asparagus in a single layer.

Using the same grater, zest a quarter of the lemon over the cheese. Grind black pepper over the zest and serve immediately.

I LOVE THIS asparagus-olive combo. Blasting the two together in a really hot oven intensifies all of the flavors. If you make this with thin asparagus spears, skip the peeling step and roast for just 6 minutes.

roasted asparagus with niçoise olives and basil   SERVES 4

2 pounds asparagus, trimmed and peeled

3 tablespoons extra-virgin olive oil, plus more for serving

Kosher salt and freshly ground black pepper

2 garlic cloves, julienned

½ cup Niçoise olives, pitted and halved

¼ cup sliced fresh basil leaves, plus more for garnish

Lemon wedges

Preheat the oven to 450°F.

Spread the asparagus in a single layer on a rimmed baking sheet. Drizzle with the oil and season with a pinch each of salt and pepper. Toss and turn to evenly coat. Sprinkle the garlic, olives, and basil all over. Roast until the asparagus is crisp-tender and the basil wilts, about 8 minutes.

Drizzle with a little more oil, garnish with fresh basil, and serve hot with lemon wedges.

MY VERSION of corn "cake" is pure corn. There's no flour, eggs, or any other binding element—the natural juices of the corn are starchy enough to hold everything together as a tender, custardy whole.

fresh corn pudding cake SERVES 4

6 to 8 large ears of corn, husks
   and silks removed
2 tablespoons unsalted butter,
   cut into small pieces
1 lime, cut into wedges
Kosher salt
Cayenne pepper

Preheat the oven to 450°F.

Grate 1 ear of corn on the large holes of a box grater over a 10-inch cast iron skillet. Grate until you reach the cob, catching all of the kernels and the corn juices in the skillet. Repeat with the remaining ears until you have an even 1½-inch-thick layer of grated corn.

Bake until a yellow skin develops on the surface, about 15 minutes; the top should not brown.

Remove from the oven and dot the surface with the butter. When the butter has melted, squeeze the juice from 1 lime wedge on top and season with salt and cayenne. Taste and adjust seasonings and serve warm with the remaining lime wedges.

I ROAST MY potatoes with garlic and herbs, so why not do the same when boiling them? I discovered that the aromatics really infuse the potatoes when you start them together in cold water and then heat them to boiling.

herbed new baby potatoes SERVES 4

1 pound new baby potatoes
   (about 16)
2 sprigs fresh thyme
2 sprigs fresh rosemary
1 large garlic clove
Kosher salt
2 tablespoons Herb Butter
   (page 139), optional

Put the potatoes in a medium saucepan and add enough cold water to cover by 2 inches. Add the thyme, rosemary, and garlic and bring to a boil over high heat. Add a generous pinch of salt, reduce the heat to medium, and cook until a knife pierces the potatoes easily, about 15 minutes.

Drain, discarding the herbs and garlic. When cool enough to handle, cut each potato in half if desired. If serving alone as a side dish, toss with the herb butter.

TOO OFTEN, summer squash ends up watery and soft. By cooking the squash on a rack, I release the water and give the squash an almost fluffy texture. The cheese creates a crisp, savory crust that makes this dish irresistible.

parmesan-crusted summer squash SERVES 4

4 small yellow summer squash, trimmed and cut at a slight angle into 1½-inch pieces

2 tablespoons extra-virgin olive oil, plus more to taste

1 teaspoon kosher salt

½ cup freshly grated Parmigiano-Reggiano cheese, plus more as needed

Lemon wedges

Fleur de sel or other coarse sea salt

Freshly ground black pepper

Preheat the oven to 375°F. Set a wire rack on a rimmed baking sheet.

In a large bowl, gently toss the squash, oil, and salt until the squash is evenly coated. Arrange the squash in a single layer on the rack, spacing the pieces at least ½ inch apart. Sprinkle the cheese evenly over the squash. Each piece should have a generous coating.

Roast until the cheese is golden brown and the edges of the squash are dark brown, about 16 minutes. Remove from the oven and let the squash cool on the rack for 10 minutes.

Use a metal spatula to transfer the squash to a serving dish. Squeeze lemon juice over the top, then drizzle with a little oil. Season with fleur de sel and pepper and serve immediately.

c'est bon The cheese causes the squash to stick to the rack. To remove the pieces, don't simply try to slide the spatula under them as you would with cookies. Instead, flip the spatula over so that the bottom is facing up. Push the edge of the spatula against the squash, the way you would scrape paint off a wall. Positioning the spatula this way creates an angle that helps lift the squash off the rack.

BLANCHING THE carrots before roasting them makes a huge difference. Not only are they more flavorful, they also become juicy and tender after roasting. Coating them with a fragrant spice paste and cooking them along with fresh citrus infuses them with an intoxicating blend of flavors.

cumin and citrus roasted carrots   SERVES 4

1 pound medium carrots, peeled
3 garlic cloves
1 teaspoon cumin seeds
1 teaspoon fresh thyme leaves
¼ teaspoon crushed red chile flakes
Kosher salt and freshly ground black pepper, plus more to taste
1 tablespoon red wine vinegar
¼ cup plus 2 tablespoons extra-virgin olive oil
1½ oranges
2 lemons, halved

Preheat the oven to 350°F.

Bring a wide pot of water to a boil. Add the carrots and cook until a knife pierces them easily, about 20 minutes.

Meanwhile, in a mortar and pestle, pound the garlic, cumin, thyme, chile, 1½ teaspoons salt, and ¾ teaspoon pepper until crushed and pasty. Add the vinegar and ¼ cup of the oil and continue pounding until well mixed. Alternatively, pulse in a food processor or blender until pasty.

Drain the carrots and arrange in a medium roasting pan in a single layer. Spoon the cumin mixture over. Cut the whole orange in half. Arrange the orange halves and 2 of the lemon halves over the carrots, cut sides down. Roast for 25 minutes or until the carrots are golden brown. Transfer the carrots to a platter.

When cool enough to handle, squeeze 2 tablespoons juice each from the roasted orange and lemon into a small bowl. Squeeze in 2 tablespoons orange juice from the remaining orange half as well as 2 tablespoons lemon juice from the remaining lemon. Whisk in the remaining 2 tablespoons oil to emulsify. Season with salt and pepper and drizzle over the carrots.

SWISS CHARD isn't exactly a bitter green, but it's not candy either. To bring out its fresh, mild, spinach-like flavor, I braise it with earthy mushrooms and thyme.

swiss chard braised in shiitake butter   SERVES 4

9 ounces Swiss chard, very
  thinly sliced crosswise
  (about 8 cups)
4 tablespoons (½ stick)
  unsalted butter
4 fresh shiitake mushroom
  caps, sliced ¼ inch thick
1 teaspoon fresh thyme leaves
Kosher salt and freshly ground
  black pepper

In a large bowl, cover the chard with cold water. Swish it around to remove all of the grit, then lift it out into a colander. Repeat if the chard is very dirty. (Don't spin it dry—you want the water clinging to the leaves.)

Heat 2 tablespoons of the butter in a large skillet over medium heat. Before the butter completely melts, add the shiitakes and thyme. Season with a little salt and cook just until fragrant, about 1 minute.

Reduce the heat to low and add the chard. Cook, gently stirring occasionally, until just tender and wilted, about 4 minutes. Raise the heat to high and cook, stirring occasionally, until the greens are very tender and almost all of the liquid has evaporated, about 3 minutes.

Add the remaining 2 tablespoons butter and cook, stirring, until the butter melts and the greens are glazed, about 3 minutes longer. Season to taste with salt and pepper and serve immediately.

THIS UNSUNG root vegetable deserves more
attention. It's sometimes called vegetable oyster or oyster plant because it actually has
a hint of that sweet brine. To highlight that unique flavor, I cook these roots in lemon
juice and toss them with a lemony beurre fondue.

salsify in lemon butter   SERVES 8

1 pound salsify, trimmed and
  peeled
2 sprigs fresh rosemary
3 stems fresh basil, leaves
  separated and sliced, stems
  reserved
¼ cup plus ⅓ cup fresh lemon
  juice
Kosher salt
5 tablespoons unsalted butter
⅛ teaspoon cayenne pepper
Freshly ground black pepper

Combine the salsify, rosemary, basil stems, ¼ cup of
the lemon juice, 1 tablespoon salt, and 2 cups water in
a large saucepan. Bring to a boil, then simmer very
gently until the salsify is tender, about 45 minutes.
Drain the salsify, and cut into 3-inch-long pieces;
halve thicker pieces lengthwise.

Combine the butter, cayenne, ½ teaspoon salt, remaining ⅓ cup lemon juice, and ⅓ cup water in a medium
saucepan. Cook over medium heat, whisking, until the
butter melts. Add the salsify and cook, stirring gently,
until the sauce thickens and clings to the salsify, about
8 minutes.

Season to taste with salt and pepper, divide among
serving plates, and top with the basil leaves.

this super-tender cabbage perfectly balances the richness of the meat. But I love it so much, I eat it on its own, too. As always with fresh cabbage, I add the juniper berries at the end to lightly perfume the dish.

sweet and sour cabbage   SERVES 4

½ cup rendered duck or
  bacon fat
1 large yellow onion, thinly
  sliced
1 (2-pound) head Savoy
  cabbage, cored and cut into
  1-inch squares
¼ cup sugar
¼ cup champagne vinegar
Kosher salt and freshly ground
  black pepper
2 cups dry Gewürztraminer
6 juniper berries, lightly
  crushed

Heat the fat in a large, wide saucepan over high heat until hot. Add the onion, reduce the heat to medium, and cook, stirring occasionally, until tender, about 8 minutes. Add the cabbage and sprinkle with the sugar and vinegar. Cook, stirring occasionally, until just tender and shiny, about 3 minutes.

Season with salt and pepper, then add the wine. Bring to a boil, cover, and cook, stirring occasionally, until the vegetables are so tender, they're almost melted, about 45 minutes. There should be just a halo of liquid left in the pan.

Stir in the juniper berries and serve.

MY GRANDMOTHER passed this recipe down to my mom and she then passed it on to me. It's a casserole of pure comfort. First, bitter endive is simmered until sweet, then wrapped in savory ham and smothered with a creamy nutmeg béchamel. Gruyère tops it off before it's baked until bubbly and golden.

braised endive with ham and gruyère SERVES 4

ENDIVE

5 tablespoons unsalted butter

¼ cup sugar

3½ tablespoons kosher salt

8 large yellow Belgian endive, trimmed

8 ounces thinly sliced Black Forest ham

BÉCHAMEL

2 tablespoons unsalted butter

¼ cup all-purpose flour

⅔ cup whole milk, warmed

1 tablespoon plus 1 teaspoon freshly grated nutmeg

¼ teaspoon freshly ground black pepper

8 ounces Gruyère cheese, shredded (1⅔ cups)

To cook the endive, combine the butter, sugar, salt, and 10½ cups water in a large pot. Bring to a boil, then reduce the heat to maintain a steady simmer. Add the endive, cover, and cook until very tender, about 45 minutes. A knife should be able to pierce through with no resistance. Use a slotted spoon to transfer the endive to paper towels. Reserve 1¼ cups cooking liquid. When cool enough to handle, squeeze out as much liquid as possible from the endive.

Wrap each endive with slices of ham. Arrange the endive in a shallow baking dish that holds them snugly; you don't want any space between the endive.

Preheat the oven to 400°F.

To make the béchamel, melt the butter in a medium saucepan over medium-low heat until golden. Add the flour and cook, whisking constantly, until the mixture smells nutty, about 2 minutes. Continue whisking and add the milk, then the reserved endive cooking liquid in a slow, steady stream. Bring the mixture to a boil while whisking. Continue whisking until thickened, about 5 minutes. Whisk in the nutmeg and pepper.

Pour the béchamel over the endive and spread to cover them evenly. Sprinkle the cheese evenly over the top. Set the dish on a rimmed baking sheet and bake until bubbly and golden brown on top, about 15 minutes. If you want the top more browned and crusty, broil for a minute or two after baking. Serve hot.

HEN OF THE woods, also known as maitake, are my favorite mushroom. They're as meaty and rich as steak and they make a great side dish. You can also try this technique with oyster mushrooms in clusters or even shiitakes, both of which will cook more quickly. The seasonings couldn't be simpler, but the unusual combination of sesame, parsley, and lime is utterly delicious.

sesame-lime roasted mushrooms SERVES 4

4 large wedges (12 ounces) hen of the woods (maitake) mushrooms
½ cup extra-virgin olive oil
Kosher salt and freshly ground black pepper
1 tablespoon white sesame seeds, toasted
2 tablespoons sliced fresh flat-leaf parsley leaves
Lime wedges, for serving

Preheat the oven to 450°F.

Put the mushrooms in a single layer on a rimmed baking sheet. Drizzle the oil all over to coat. Season generously with salt and pepper. Roast until the edges are browned and crispy, the outer edges tender, and a knife encounters some resistance when piercing the center, about 20 minutes.

Transfer to a serving dish. Sprinkle the sesame seeds and parsley over the mushrooms and serve with the lime wedges.

I CAME UP with this technique of boiling a squash whole while watching a movie. I didn't want to miss the good parts—and the kids didn't want to pause it for me while I tended the stove. The squash ended up cooking beautifully, becoming juicy and tender with zero effort.

butternut squash with balsamic and chile panko crumbs SERVES 8

1 large butternut squash (about 2½ pounds)

2 tablespoons balsamic vinegar

5 tablespoons extra-virgin olive oil

Kosher salt and freshly ground black pepper

1 cup panko crumbs

1½ teaspoons fresh thyme leaves

½ teaspoon crushed red chile flakes

¼ cup freshly grated Parmigiano-Reggiano cheese

Bring a large stockpot of water to a boil. Add the whole squash and cook, partially covered, until tender, about 45 minutes. (A knife will pierce the flesh very easily.) Drain, cool slightly, then remove and discard the stem and peel. Reserve the seeds, removing and discarding the strings.

Transfer the flesh to a large serving dish and mash with a fork into an even layer. Drizzle the vinegar and 2 tablespoons of the oil over the squash, and season with salt and pepper.

Heat 3 tablespoons of the squash seeds in a large skillet over medium-low heat until dry. Add 1 tablespoon of the oil and a pinch of salt and toast, tossing occasionally. When the seeds begin to pop, partially cover the pan. Continue toasting until golden brown, about 3 minutes, then transfer to a plate.

In the same skillet, heat the remaining 2 tablespoons oil over medium heat, then toss in the crumbs. When well coated, stir in the thyme, chile, and ¼ teaspoon salt. Toast, tossing occasionally, until golden brown and fragrant, about 5 minutes. Remove from the heat and stir in the cheese and toasted seeds. Spread the crumb mixture over the squash in an even layer and serve immediately.

AS A RULE, I season my greens in direct proportion to their degree of bitterness. To mellow the edge of mustard greens without overwhelming them with seasoning, I use this technique of cooking them in salty boiling water with butter melted into it. It infuses the greens with tons of flavor, but keeps their natural edge intact. If you love that hot, mustardy bite, be sure to add the mustard oil at the end.

butter-blanched mustard greens SERVES 4

1 pound mustard greens
12 tablespoons (1½ sticks) unsalted butter
⅓ cup kosher salt, plus more to taste
Mustard oil, optional (see Pantry, page 253)
Freshly ground black pepper

Remove and discard the ribs of the mustard greens. Cut the leaves into ¼-inch strips. Wash and dry the leaves well.

Meanwhile, in a large pot, bring 6 cups water to a boil. Add the butter and salt and return to a rapid boil. Add the greens and cook, stirring, until wilted and tender, about 4 minutes. Drain and transfer to a serving dish.

Drizzle with a little mustard oil, if you like, and season with salt and pepper.

TO BRING OUT the best in this snowy white root
vegetable, I simmer it in honey and citrus. A little heat balances the luscious sweetness.

honey-glazed parsnips SERVES 4

2 pounds parsnips, trimmed,
  peeled, and cut into
  5 × 1-inch batons
2 cups fresh orange juice
½ cup fresh lime juice
3 tablespoons honey
10 tablespoons unsalted butter
Grated zest of 2 limes
½ fresh red Thai chile, thinly
  sliced
Kosher salt

In a large sauté pan, combine the parsnips, orange juice, 1 cup water, the lime juice, honey, butter, lime zest, and chile. Season with salt, cover, and bring to a boil over medium heat. Simmer over low heat for 20 minutes. Uncover and simmer, gently stirring occasionally, until the parsnips are very tender and glazed, about 15 minutes longer.

desserts

I HAVE A SERIOUS SWEET TOOTH. Every night, before bed, I need a piece of chocolate. (And then again when I wake up in the morning.) Of course, I don't actually prepare dessert every day. If Chloe wants something sweet on a school night, I cut up some fruit and serve it with yogurt. But on the weekends, I make sure we have at least one dessert. My mom and grandmother were both excellent bakers and specialized in buttery tarts. For me, tarts are a taste of home. I love serving them freshly baked and still barely cooled. The sort of sharing at the table required with a tart—by taking a slice from the whole—is very important to me.

What my mom and grandmother taught me—aside from the importance of not overworking the dough—is that making desserts is as much an art as it is a science. That is, it's as much about the feel of the dough as getting the measurements right. It's just as important to use the best cultured butter possible; I prefer Vermont Creamery. If you can't find that, look for a good European high-fat butter.

Of course, they also taught me that it's a true joy to transform butter, sugar, and flour into crowd-pleasing creations. As familiar and comforting as the flavors may be, they still surprise too. For example, I put a pear claufouti filling into a tart shell. To add another twist, I caramelize the fruit in honey first. What looks like a simple custardy tart actually has layers of flavors that everyone loves. That's the end goal: to make original desserts that taste really great.

IN THIS SIMPLE dessert, fresh fruit is the star. Lemon juice brings out the sweetness of summer cherries and berries. Any red berries work here—fresh red currants, black currants, and gooseberries are great options, too.

berries in fresh cherry syrup   SERVES 4

1 pound Bing cherries, pitted
½ cup sugar
1 pound strawberries, hulled
  and halved
1 pint raspberries
½ pint blueberries
1 tablespoon fresh lemon juice
Lemon sorbet, fromage blanc,
  or whipped cream, for
  serving

Combine the cherries, sugar, and 1½ cups water in a large saucepan. Cover and bring to a boil over high heat. Lower the heat and simmer, stirring occasionally, until the cherries soften, about 10 minutes.

Transfer to a large bowl and let cool to room temperature. Gently stir in the strawberries, raspberries, blueberries, and lemon juice. Let stand for at least 30 minutes or refrigerate, covered, for up to 1 day.

Serve topped with lemon sorbet, fromage blanc, or whipped cream.

THIS IS A dessert I serve all year round with whatever fruit is ripe. I always include orange segments though, as a reminder of the citrus in the sabayon sauce. You can make each serving of this dessert as small or large as you want, depending on how much fruit you use. In its simplicity, *c'est bon!*

seasonal fruit gratin with citrus sabayon SERVES 4

3 large egg yolks
¼ cup sugar
⅓ cup fresh orange juice
Sliced fresh fruit, such as
    oranges, berries, peaches,
    apricots, pineapple, papaya,
    passion fruit, star fruit,
    or mango

Arrange an oven rack 6 inches below the broiler heat source. Preheat the broiler.

Fill a medium saucepan with an inch of water. Bring to a boil, then lower the heat to maintain a bare simmer.

Whisk the yolks in a heatproof bowl until broken. Whisk in the sugar until well blended, then whisk in the orange juice. Set the bowl over (but not touching) the simmering water and whisk constantly and rapidly until the mixture becomes pale yellow and thick, about 6 minutes. Remove from the heat.

Divide the fruit among 4 shallow gratin dishes. Spoon the sabayon over the fruit. Broil until just golden brown, about 1 minute. (Be careful: It goes from golden to black fast!) Serve immediately.

THIS RECIPE comes straight from my home in Alsace. My mom didn't always have time to make fresh pastry cream, so she combined homemade strawberry jam, which we kept on hand, with *fraises des bois.* Those tiny, wild, sweet strawberries pair perfectly with the almond and vanilla sablé dough.

fresh strawberry tart   SERVES 8

Almond Sablé dough
   (page 216)
⅔ cup plus 1 tablespoon
   strawberry jam, preferably
   homemade
2 pounds small strawberries,
   preferably wild, stemmed

Form the dough into a disk and roll it between 2 sheets of parchment paper or plastic wrap. Carefully transfer it to a 10-inch round fluted tart pan with a removable bottom. Use your palm to gently press the dough into the bottom of the pan, then use your fingers to press it up the sides, patching any holes or tears that form. Refrigerate the dough for 30 minutes.

While the dough chills, preheat the oven to 350°F.

Bake the chilled dough until browned and crisp, about 30 minutes. Let cool completely on a wire rack.

Spread ⅔ cup of the jam evenly over the bottom of the dough. Arrange the strawberries in concentric circles to cover the bottom, then top with another layer of strawberries.

When ready to serve, heat the remaining 1 tablespoon jam with 1 tablespoon water until just bubbling. Brush all over the strawberries. Remove the tart ring and serve immediately.

WHEN I WAS an apprentice, I had to perfect a four-star version of this classic dessert. It was painfully involved and difficult. Over the years, I discovered that I much prefer a more rustic take. The fundamentals remain the same, and I still love the Tatin technique. The sound of the buttery caramel sizzling is music to my ears. Serve this with a little crème fraîche, and life is beautiful.

tarte tatin SERVES 8

All-purpose flour
1 (9-ounce) sheet frozen all-butter puff pastry, thawed
7 tablespoons unsalted butter, preferably cultured, at room temperature
½ cup sugar
8 to 10 Granny Smith apples (7½ pounds), peeled, halved, and cored
Crème fraîche, for serving

Using a lightly floured rolling pin, roll the puff pastry on a lightly floured work surface into a 10-inch round. Transfer to a cookie sheet and freeze until firm.

Preheat the oven to 400°F.

Mash together the butter and sugar in an ovenproof nonstick 10-inch skillet with your fingers. Pat into an even layer covering the bottom of the pan.

Arrange the apple halves upright in concentric circles around the pan; they should fit very snugly. If necessary, cut some halves into quarters to fill in any gaps.

Set the pan over high heat and cook, turning the pan occasionally for even browning, until the caramel bubbles rapidly and becomes medium-dark amber around the edges and on the bottom. Carefully transfer to the oven and bake until the apples become very soft, about 20 minutes.

Top with the puff pastry and bake until puffed and brown, about 15 minutes. Let cool to room temperature, about 1 hour.

When ready to serve, warm over medium heat to loosen the tarte from the pan, about 1 minute. Center a serving plate over the pan and carefully invert the plate and skillet. Remove the skillet, cut the tarte into wedges, and serve with crème fraîche.

I LOVE CLAFOUTI, especially with ripe pears, but I always felt something was missing. To make a great French dessert even better, I added a buttery crust. That thin, crisp layer makes a world of difference. Tender pears soaked with caramelized honey do, too.

honeyed pear clafouti tart   SERVES 8

Shortbread dough (page 217)
5 tablespoons clover honey
8 very small or 4 medium
    pears, peeled, quartered,
    and cored
2 large eggs
2 large egg yolks

½ cup granulated sugar
3 tablespoons cornstarch
1 cup heavy cream
1 cup sliced blanched almonds
Confectioners' sugar, for
    serving

Preheat the oven to 375°F.

Form the shortbread dough into a disk and center in a 10-inch-round fluted tart pan with a removable bottom. Use your palm to gently press the dough into the bottom of the pan, then use your fingers to press it up the sides. (The dough will be very thin.) Refrigerate the dough for 5 minutes.

Bake until golden brown, about 15 minutes.

Meanwhile, heat the honey in a large nonstick skillet over medium heat until bubbling. Add the pears in a single layer and cook, carefully turning the fruit, until they're almost translucent and very tender, about 7 minutes. Almost all of the honey will have evaporated.

Whisk together the eggs, yolks, and granulated sugar until pale and foamy. Whisk in the cornstarch until no lumps remain, then whisk in the cream until the mixture is smooth.

Arrange the pears in the crust in a single layer, then pour the egg mixture over them. The tart shell will be very full. Sprinkle the almonds on top. Bake until the custard is set and the top is dark brown, about 20 minutes. Let cool completely on a wire rack, then remove the tart ring.

Dust with confectioners' sugar and serve immediately.

I LOVE THIS natural fruit-nut pairing and how the apricot juices run right into the frangipane filling.

apricot frangipane tart   SERVES 6

1 (9-ounce) sheet frozen all-
    butter puff pastry, thawed
All-purpose flour
4 tablespoons (½ stick)
    unsalted butter, preferably
    cultured, softened
½ cup confectioners' sugar,
    plus more for dusting
½ cup almond flour
1 large egg, at room
    temperature
12 small apricots (2 pounds),
    halved and pitted

Preheat the oven to 350°F.

Roll the puff pastry on a lightly floured work surface into an 11-inch round. Fit it into an 8-inch round fluted tart pan with a removable bottom. Press the dough ½ inch above the rim of the pan, trimming excess. Freeze until firm.

Use a fork to poke holes all over the bottom of the dough. Line with foil, fill with pie weights, and bake until dry to the touch, about 15 minutes. Remove the foil and weights and bake for 10 minutes longer or until golden. Let cool completely on a wire rack.

Whisk together the butter and confectioners' sugar until well combined. Add the almond flour and egg and whisk until blended and fluffy. Spread in an even layer in the cooled crust.

Arrange the apricots in concentric circles, sitting upright with the cut sides at a slight angle. Bake until browned, about 50 minutes. Let cool completely. Remove the tart ring, dust with confectioners' sugar, and serve.

IN FRENCH, *sablé* means "sand," and that's the
texture you're aiming for here. Avoid overworking the dough to prevent it from
becoming tough. I love its light, crisp, and crumbly texture in tarts and on its own.

almond sablés

MAKES ONE 10-INCH TART OR ABOUT 1 DOZEN COOKIES

5 tablespoons unsalted butter,
preferably cultured, at room
temperature

⅓ cup plus 2 tablespoons sifted
confectioners' sugar

1 large egg yolk

½ vanilla bean, split lengthwise

¾ cup all-purpose flour

3 tablespoons almond flour

⅛ teaspoon kosher salt

Combine the butter and ⅓ cup of the confectioners'
sugar on your work surface. Use your fingers to gently
massage the butter into the sugar until well combined.
Form into a mound with a well in the center.

Put the yolk in the well and scrape the seeds from the
vanilla bean on top. (Save the pod for another use.) Use
your fingers to incorporate the yolk and vanilla into
the butter.

Sift the flours, salt, and remaining 2 tablespoons confectioners' sugar over the butter mixture. Use your
fingers to gradually draw the flour mixture into the
butter mixture. Gently mix until combined and large
clumps just begin to form. The dough should hold
together if you squeeze some.

Use the dough to make a tart crust as on page 209, or
bake into cookies: Form the dough into a log. Wrap
tightly in plastic wrap and refrigerate until firm or
freeze for up to 1 month; if frozen, thaw overnight in
the refrigerator before baking.

Preheat the oven to 350°F.

Cut the log into ¼-inch-thick slices and arrange on
an ungreased cookie sheet, spacing the rounds 1 inch
apart. Bake until golden brown and crisp, about 10 minutes. Let cool completely on a wire rack.

TARTS ARE THE desserts of my childhood. One of their appeals for me is that they can be filled with whatever you like. My good friend Magnus Hansson, a masterful baker, recently shared his foolproof shortbread recipe with me. It's the base of my Honeyed Pear Clafouti Tart (page 212), but I fill it with everything from pastry cream to caramelized nuts.

shortbread

MAKES ONE 10-INCH TART OR ABOUT 1 DOZEN COOKIES

6 tablespoons (¾ stick) unsalted butter, preferably cultured, at room temperature

3 tablespoons sugar

¼ teaspoon vanilla extract

¾ cup all-purpose flour

Grated zest of ¼ lemon

¼ teaspoon kosher salt

Beat the butter, sugar, and vanilla in a mixer with the paddle attachment on medium speed just until mixed together, about 1 minute. Add the flour, zest, and salt. Beat on low speed just until the dough forms a ball.

Use the dough to make a tart crust as on page 213, or bake into cookies: Form the ball of dough into a log. Wrap tightly in plastic wrap and refrigerate until firm or freeze for up to 1 month; if frozen, thaw overnight in the refrigerator before baking.

Preheat the oven to 350°F.

Cut the log into ¼-inch-thick slices and arrange on an ungreased cookie sheet, spacing the rounds 1 inch apart. Bake until golden brown and crisp, about 8 minutes. Let cool completely on a wire rack.

c'est bon If desired, roll the log of dough in raw sugar or chopped nuts before freezing to add a nice texture and flavor to the finished cookies.

ONE AFTERNOON, I was craving chocolate mousse, but didn't want to mess with eggs. I came up with this super-easy version. Temperature is key here: The cream should be thick and very cold when you whisk in the slightly cooled liquid chocolate. If the cream isn't cold enough and the chocolate's too hot, the mixture will melt. If the cream is too cold and the chocolate has cooled too much, the chocolate will solidify. You also want to avoid overwhipping the cream to keep this dessert luscious and creamy. Even if you don't nail the texture the first time, it'll still be delicious. What's not to love about chocolate and cream?

bittersweet chocolate chantilly SERVES 4

1½ cups heavy cream
3½ ounces bittersweet
   chocolate, preferably
   Valrhona 71% cacao, finely
   chopped, plus additional
   for garnish

Whisk the cream in a large metal bowl until thick but before soft peaks form. Transfer to the freezer.

Fill a medium saucepan with an inch of water and bring to a simmer. Put the chocolate in a large heat-proof bowl and set over the saucepan; do not let the bottom of the bowl touch the water. Melt the chocolate, stirring occasionally, then remove from the heat. Let cool. The chocolate should be cool and liquid and not yet solidified.

Whisk the cold cream continuously while adding the chocolate in a slow, steady stream. When the chocolate is fully incorporated, freeze the mixture for 2 minutes. Divide among 4 serving bowls and let stand for a few minutes before serving. Shave chocolate over the chantilly for garnish.

NO, THIS IS *not* my famous molten chocolate cake. While I'm glad the molten cake is as popular as it is, this simple cake is the dessert of choice in my home. It's Chloe's favorite, and mine, too. My mom used to make this for me as an after-school treat. Very, very moist, it's like a brownie and tastes even better after it sits for a day.

chocolate cake   SERVES 6

4 tablespoons (½ stick) unsalted butter, preferably cultured, plus more for the pan

1 tablespoon all-purpose flour, plus more for the pan

3 large eggs, separated

1 teaspoon granulated sugar

3½ ounces bittersweet chocolate, preferably Valrhona 66% cacao, chopped

½ cup confectioners' sugar

½ cup almond flour

Dutch-process cocoa powder, optional

Preheat the oven to 350°F. Butter and flour an 8-inch round fluted tart pan with a removable bottom or a springform pan, tapping out the excess.

Whisk the egg whites with the granulated sugar until medium-stiff peaks form.

Meanwhile, fill a medium saucepan with an inch of water and bring to a simmer. Combine the chocolate and butter in a heatproof bowl and set over the simmering water. Melt, stirring occasionally. Remove the bowl from the saucepan.

Beat 1 yolk into the chocolate mixture to temper it. Beat in the remaining yolks, then beat in the confectioners' sugar, almond flour, and all-purpose flour until well mixed.

Add a third of the whipped whites and beat well to loosen the chocolate mixture. Gently fold in the remaining whites just until combined. Pour into the prepared pan and gently spread evenly.

Bake until puffed and a knife comes out clean, about 17 minutes. Let cool in the pan on a wire rack for 10 minutes, then invert onto the rack. Carefully flip the cake right side up. Let cool completely. Dust with cocoa powder if you like.

brunch

EVERY WEEKEND, I START PREPARING brunch as soon as I walk in the door of our country house. I'm always armed with at least a dozen eggs from John Boy's Farm Market. The eggs' pale green shells are beautiful, but it's their dark ochre yolks that are really gorgeous—and delicious. They're so fresh, they remind me of the eggs we had growing up. I like to fry them, turn them into perfect omelets, poach them. Any way they're prepared, they're the perfect start to the weekend—that and a good cup of coffee with milk from Meadow Brook Farms Dairy.

The family trickles in on Saturday mornings, so I make big brunch dishes to share. I definitely don't cook *à la carte* on the weekends. It's more fun to set all the dishes out on the counter and have everyone choose what they want. Chloe and her cousins love pancakes, especially when I make my homemade toppings with seasonal fruit. Brioche French toast is always a hit, too.

I prefer Sunday morning brunches at the table. I'm usually the first one up and I start cooking as soon as I'm out of bed. I set the table and prepare a spread for everyone in the house. We all sit down together for eggs, of course, maybe something sweet like coffee cake, and really good bread. In the city, I pick up sourdough from Balthazar or Sullivan Street Bakery and get bagels from H & H. Artisan bakery bread is always worth the splurge. Even on weekdays, when I don't have time for a leisurely morning meal, a good slice of multigrain toast is all I need.

I STARTED shopping in supermarkets only after we got our country house and I needed to stock the kitchen there. When I went into the Whole Foods near my flagship restaurant, I was astounded by everything they sell. They have a machine that lets you make your own almond butter! I like to grind it so that it's almost smooth but still a bit chunky. On grainy bakery bread with bananas, it's heaven. This is what I eat for breakfast every morning. It's best with a cup of hot coffee.

seven-grain toast with almond butter and banana SERVES 1

1 slice 7-grain bread
1 banana
2 tablespoons almond butter

Toast the bread until golden. Meanwhile, slice the banana ¼ inch thick at an angle. Spread the almond butter on the warm toast and layer the banana slices on top.

THIS IS THE ultimate French toast. It's more like dessert, with the crème anglaise and caramel, but one well worth having in the morning. To achieve the perfect balance between crisp outside and custard center, you must completely soak the bread.

french toast with roasted apples SERVES 4

⅔ cup whole milk

⅔ cup heavy cream

½ cup sugar

1 large egg

1 large egg yolk

⅓ vanilla bean, split lengthwise and seeds scraped, pod reserved for another use

4 (1-inch-thick) slices brioche, preferably day-old

3 tablespoons unsalted butter, plus more for the pan

2 Golden Delicious apples, peeled, cored, and cut into eighths

Crème Anglaise (page 251), optional

Caramel Sauce (page 251), optional

Confectioners' sugar

Whisk together the milk, cream, sugar, egg, yolk, and vanilla bean seeds until the sugar dissolves. Arrange the brioche slices in a single layer in a shallow baking dish. Pour the milk-egg mixture over the bread, submerging the bread. Cover with plastic wrap and refrigerate until the bread is completely soaked and almost too soft to handle, at least 1 hour and up to overnight.

When you're almost ready to serve, preheat the oven to 400°F. Generously butter a small rimmed baking sheet. Arrange the apples in a single layer. Dot the apples with 1 tablespoon of the butter. Roast until golden brown and tender, about 10 minutes.

Meanwhile, melt the remaining 2 tablespoons butter in a large ovenproof nonstick skillet over medium-low heat. When the butter foams, use both hands to very carefully transfer the soaked brioche slices to the pan. Cook until golden brown, about 5 minutes, then carefully flip. Transfer to the oven and bake alongside the apples until golden brown and puffed, about 5 minutes.

Serve the French toast with the apples and the crème anglaise and caramel, if desired. Dust with confectioners' sugar

ONE SUMMER morning, I decided to make good use of the ripe stone fruit I had picked up at the farmer's market. I didn't have any brioche at home, but I did have a loaf of sourdough. It turned out that the tanginess of the bread was delicious with the sweet fruit. And amaretto adds just the right hint of almond.

stone fruit bruschetta SERVES 4

4 ripe apricots, pitted and cut into thin wedges

4 ripe Italian plums, pitted and cut into thin wedges

2 ripe peaches, pitted and cut into thin wedges

2 ripe nectarines, pitted and cut into thin wedges

1 vanilla bean, split lengthwise and seeds scraped

⅓ cup sugar

2 tablespoons amaretto

Unsalted butter, preferably cultured, at room temperature

4 slices good sourdough bread

Toss the apricots, plums, peaches, nectarines, vanilla seeds and pod, sugar, and amaretto in a large bowl until the sugar dissolves. Let stand for at least 20 minutes, but preferably for 2 hours.

Preheat the oven to 350°F. Generously butter a small rimmed baking sheet.

Generously butter one side of each slice of bread. Arrange buttered side up in a single layer in the pan. Spoon the fruit and their juices over the bread. Be sure to get a nice mix of colors on each slice. Bake until the bread is browned and crisp and the fruit tender, about 10 minutes. Serve immediately.

c'est bon Cut plums as you do mangoes, running the knife down along the pits. That makes it easy to slice them into neat wedges.

CHLOE'S FAVORITE breakfast dish has become mine, too. I wouldn't trade our weekend ritual of whisking the batter together for anything.

buttermilk pancakes   SERVES 4

½ cup all-purpose flour
½ teaspoon baking soda
¼ teaspoon kosher salt
1 cup buttermilk
1 large egg
3 tablespoons unsalted butter, melted, plus more for the pan
Warm Berry Syrup (recipe follows)
Confectioners' sugar

In a large bowl, whisk together the flour, baking soda, and salt. In a small bowl, whisk together the buttermilk and egg, then pour into the flour mixture. Whisk until just combined, then whisk in the butter until just incorporated. (The batter should be a little lumpy.) Let the batter rest at room temperature for 10 to 15 minutes.

When ready to cook, heat a nonstick skillet or griddle over medium heat. When hot, lightly butter the pan, then pour in a scant ¼ cup batter. Repeat, pouring the batter a few inches apart and working in batches. Cook until bubbles pop on the surface of each pancake, 3 to 4 minutes, then flip and cook for 1 minute more.

Arrange the pancakes on plates, top with the syrup, dust with confectioners' sugar, and serve immediately.

warm berry syrup MAKES 3 CUPS

In spring, I like to make my own syrup in lieu of maple syrup, which I prefer in the fall and winter. The first berries of the season, which aren't very sweet, are transformed by the golden caramel that melts into the firm fruit.

¼ cup sugar
2 tablespoons unsalted butter, at room temperature
1½ cups hulled and quartered strawberries
1 cup blueberries
1 cup raspberries

Combine the sugar and ¼ cup water in a large skillet. Bring the mixture to a boil over medium-high heat, stirring to dissolve the sugar. Boil, undisturbed, for 2 minutes. Stir in the butter and boil until golden and fragrant, about 3 minutes.

Add all of the berries to the skillet and cook, stirring gently to coat the fruit, until the caramel melts into the fruit and the berries begin to release their juices, about 3 minutes. Serve warm.

ONE SATURDAY, Greg Brainin, my director of creative development, threw this together for his daughters. When he made it for me the following Monday, I knew it would become a regular weekend treat for my family, too. It's as comforting as a classic buttery coffee cake, but the crunch of raw sugar and sea salt in the topping makes it taste refreshingly new.

greg's blueberry crumble cake   SERVES 8

BLUEBERRY CAKE

6 tablespoons (¾ stick) unsalted butter, preferably cultured, melted, plus more for the pan

⅓ cup buttermilk, at room temperature

1 large egg, at room temperature

1 large egg yolk, at room temperature

⅓ vanilla bean, split lengthwise and seeds scraped, pod reserved for another use

1½ cups all-purpose flour

¾ cup granulated sugar

1½ teaspoons baking powder

¾ teaspoon kosher salt

1 pint blueberries

SPICED CRUMBLE TOPPING

½ cup all-purpose flour

3 tablespoons granulated sugar

1 teaspoon ground cinnamon

¼ teaspoon ground allspice

3 tablespoons unsalted butter, preferably cultured, cut up and chilled

1 tablespoon raw sugar

1 teaspoon Maldon salt or other flaky sea salt

To make the cake, preheat the oven to 375°F. Butter a 9 × 5-inch nonstick loaf pan.

In a medium bowl, whisk together the buttermilk, egg, yolk, and vanilla seeds until well blended. Continue whisking while drizzling in the butter.

In a large bowl, whisk together the flour, sugar, baking powder, and salt. Add the buttermilk mixture and whisk until just blended. Use a rubber spatula to fold in the blueberries. Transfer to the prepared pan, smoothing the top.

To make the topping, whisk together the flour, granulated sugar, cinnamon, and allspice in a medium bowl. Rub in the butter using your fingers until the mixture is crumbly with a few pea-sized pieces remaining. Sprinkle evenly over the cake batter. Sprinkle the raw sugar and Maldon salt evenly over the topping.

Bake until deep golden brown and a tester inserted in the center of the cake comes out clean, about 1 hour. Let cool completely in the pan on a wire rack. Unmold and cut into slices to serve.

WHEN WE HAVE a lot of people over for brunch, I love serving my version of a New York classic. Each person can easily pick up a stack—only half a bagel—from a tower and not get full on too much bread. You can even cut each tower into quarters so your guests can pick up a bite. I like using H&H poppy seed bagels, but feel free to substitute your favorite bagel.

towers of bagel toasts, smoked salmon, and herbs SERVES 8

4 bagels

1 (8-ounce) package cream cheese, at room temperature

1 pound thinly sliced smoked salmon

½ cup chopped fresh herb leaves, preferably dill, parsley, and basil

Carefully cut each bagel horizontally into 4 even slices; each round will be ¼ to ½ inch thick. Toast until golden and crisp.

You then reassemble each bagel: Spread cream cheese on the 2 bottom halves (the rounded bottom and the upper-middle slice) of each bagel. Top each cream cheese slice with 2 slices of smoked salmon and 2 tablespoons herbs. Top with the other bagel slice and reassemble each bagel. Cut in half or quarters if you like.

I CONSIDER myself a pretty high-energy guy, but some mornings, even I need something that will really wake me up. The fresh ginger and pinch of salt brighten the fresh fruit and vegetable juices here, making this an ideal breakfast drink. It also cures a hangover like nothing else. Or so I'm told . . .

carrot, orange, and ginger
eye-opener SERVES 4

1½ cups fresh carrot juice

¾ cup fresh orange juice

¾ cup fresh passion fruit juice

¾ cup plain whole-milk yogurt

2-inch piece fresh ginger,
   peeled and chopped

2 tablespoons sugar

½ teaspoon kosher salt

Combine the juices, yogurt, ginger, sugar, and salt in a blender. Puree until smooth. Serve chilled.

WHEN I FIRST moved to America I had never tasted eggs Benedict before and was shocked by its popularity. Over the years, I've made this dish my own. Most hollandaise recipes call for clarified butter, but I prefer using fresh butter to capture the rich milk flavor.

eggs benedict SERVES 4

2 large egg yolks, at room
  temperature
Kosher salt
8 tablespoons (1 stick) unsalted
  butter, at room temperature
¼ teaspoon cayenne pepper
1 teaspoon fresh lemon juice
1 teaspoon white wine vinegar
4 large eggs
2 English muffins, split
4 slices very good ham
1 teaspoon minced fresh chives
Freshly ground black pepper

Combine the yolks, 2 tablespoons water, and a pinch of salt in a medium saucepan. Set over medium heat and whisk constantly and rapidly until the mixture becomes very thick, about 4 minutes.

Remove from the heat and add the butter, a little at a time, while whisking rapidly, until incorporated. Set over medium heat and whisk for 1 minute longer. Whisk in the cayenne, a pinch of salt, and the lemon juice. Keep warm over very low heat.

Fill a medium shallow saucepan halfway with water. Bring to a boil and add the vinegar and a generous pinch of salt. Reduce the heat to maintain a simmer.

Line a plate with several layers of paper towels. Break an egg into a bowl, hold the rim of the bowl close to the water, and slide in the egg. Repeat with the remaining eggs. Cook just until the whites are set, but the yolks are still runny, 3 to 4 minutes. Use a slotted spoon to carefully transfer each egg to the paper towels to drain. Trim the edges if you'd like. Meanwhile, toast the English muffins in a broiler or toaster oven until golden brown. Place a slice of ham on top of each and toast just a little longer to warm the ham.

Set each muffin half on a plate. Arrange a poached egg on top of the ham. Spoon the hollandaise over. Garnish with chives, grind pepper over the top, and serve.

c'est bon You can use smoked salmon, or even sautéed spinach, in place of the ham.

ONE OF MY first lessons as an apprentice, both in my mom's kitchen and in my first restaurant position, was how to perfect an omelet. It should be fluffy, with runny eggs, and never browned. Back then, we used steel pans. We now have the advantage of nonstick pans, which make the technique more foolproof and the omelet every bit as delicious. Although the chiles are optional, they're my favorite part of this dish. They add a bright note to accent the wilted spinach and creamy goat cheese melted into the eggs.

spinach and cheese omelet with pickled red chiles   SERVES 2

2 teaspoons extra-virgin olive oil

15 ounces fresh spinach leaves (5 cups packed)

Kosher salt and freshly ground black pepper

6 large eggs

2 tablespoons unsalted butter

¼ cup crumbled fresh goat cheese

1 tablespoon Pickled Long Red Chiles (page 248), optional

Heat the oil in a large nonstick skillet over medium heat. Add the spinach and season with a small pinch of salt. Cook, stirring, until just wilted. Transfer to paper towels to drain and dry. Wipe out the skillet.

Whisk the eggs with a generous pinch each of salt and pepper. Melt the butter in the skillet over medium heat, swirling the pan to coat evenly. When it foams, add the eggs. Cook, shaking the pan while stirring with a rubber spatula, until small curds form and are suspended in the runny mixture. Cook, undisturbed, just until the edges are set. Remove from the heat.

Sprinkle the spinach and goat cheese all over the eggs. Use the spatula to carefully fold the omelet in half while tilting the skillet. Tip the omelet out of the skillet onto a plate. Top with the chiles, if you like, and cut in half to share. Serve immediately.

THIS DISH IS more or less fried eggs with crunchy, savory bits cooked into them. It's like a cross between a frittata and an omelet, but a whole lot better. This is Marja's favorite weekend breakfast, so I usually just make two servings for us to share, but you can easily double the recipe below if you cook it in a large skillet.

fried eggs with crisp croutons, bacon, and asparagus SERVES 2

4 slices bacon, preferably
   double-smoked, cut
   crosswise into ½-inch pieces
1 slice sourdough bread, crusts
   removed, cut into ½-inch
   dice (½ cup)
2 large asparagus spears,
   trimmed and sliced ⅛ inch
   thick at an angle
Kosher salt
1 white new (spring) onion
   or scallion, white and pale
   green parts only, thinly
   sliced at an angle
4 large eggs
1 tablespoon thinly sliced fresh
   long red (finger) chile
1 tablespoon chopped fresh
   dill

Cook the bacon in a medium nonstick skillet over medium-high heat, stirring occasionally to separate the pieces, until golden and the fat is rendered, 2 to 3 minutes. Add the bread and asparagus and season with a small pinch of salt. Cook, stirring occasionally, until the bacon and bread are evenly browned and crisp, about 7 minutes. Stir in the onion and cook until tender and fragrant, about 2 minutes.

Break the eggs into the pan, letting the whites run together. When the bottom just sets, sprinkle the chile, dill, and a small pinch of salt over the eggs. Cook until the whites are set and the yolks runny, 3 to 4 minutes. Serve hot.

YES, THIS IS good for you. But that's not the reason I eat it. By whipping the egg whites just until foamy, the resulting omelet is light and delicious. (Unwhisked egg whites get rubbery.) Unlike regular omelets, which shouldn't color, this one gets cooked in a blazing hot pan until crisped and brown and the fresh herbs get sealed right into the whites. While lemon may seem an unlikely pairing for eggs, the bit of zest at the end adds a brightness perfect for the clean flavors here.

egg white omelet with fines herbes SERVES 2

4 large egg whites
2 tablespoons coarsely chopped
    fresh herb leaves, preferably
    a mix of mint, parsley,
    chives, and tarragon, plus
    more for garnish
Kosher salt
Extra-virgin olive oil
Freshly ground black pepper
1 lemon
Scotch Bonnet Hot Sauce
    (page 248), optional

Beat the egg whites until foamy on top. Beat in half of the herbs and season with salt.

Heat a large nonstick skillet over high heat until very hot. Add enough oil to coat the bottom of the skillet. When very hot, add the egg mixture, swirling the pan to spread it in an even, thin layer.

Cook until crisp and golden brown on the bottom, about 1 minute. Sprinkle the remaining herbs over, then remove from the heat and immediately use 2 spatulas to fold the omelet in half while tilting the skillet. (It's okay if the whites aren't totally set; the residual heat will cook them.)

Slide onto a serving plate and drizzle with a little olive oil. Grind pepper over and grate the zest of a quarter of the lemon directly over the omelet. Garnish with herbs. Cut in half to share. Serve immediately, with hot sauce, if you like.

basics

ginger syrup

MAKES ABOUT 1 CUP

THIS IS POSSIBLY one of the most versatile building blocks I've ever made. This syrup has found itself into hundreds of my recipes because of its balance of sweetness, heat, and acid. Over the years, I've tweaked the mix, changing the acid, adding aromatics. For now, the formula below is what I'm sticking with. Originally conceived as the base for homemade Ginger Lemon Soda (page 25), it quickly became my go-to syrup for spritzers.

1 cup peeled and chopped fresh ginger
1 cup sugar
1 cup fresh lemon juice

Combine the ginger, sugar, and lemon juice in a small saucepan. Bring to a boil, stirring to dissolve the sugar. Remove from the heat and let cool to room temperature. Strain through a sieve into a container, pressing on the ginger; discard the ginger. The syrup can be covered and refrigerated for up to 3 days.

red wine citrus vinaigrette

MAKES ABOUT ⅔ CUP

WHILE I USE this to dress my chicken salad (page 130), I also like it on soft bitter lettuces. Too often, we relegate vinaigrettes to greens, but they're also good with proteins. This one, in particular, pairs well with salmon, either poached or slow-baked.

1 tablespoon minced shallot
¼ teaspoon minced fresh Thai chile
3 tablespoons plus 1 teaspoon fresh orange juice
2 tablespoons fresh lemon juice
2 tablespoons red wine vinegar
1 tablespoon kosher salt
3 tablespoons plus 2 teaspoons extra-virgin olive oil

In a medium bowl, whisk together the shallot, chile, juices, vinegar, and salt until the salt dissolves. Continue whisking while adding the oil in a slow, steady stream. The dressing can be covered and refrigerated overnight.

house dressing

MAKES ABOUT ¾ CUP

TRUFFLE JUICE, an amazing ingredient that truly captures the heady aroma and taste of freshly harvested truffles, pairs well with soy sauce because they both have a rich earthiness. That depth of flavor makes this a natural pairing for other savory ingredients, like mushrooms and steak. Any salad with Parmesan cheese would benefit from a drizzle of this dressing, too.

2 tablespoons truffle juice
  (see Pantry, page 253)
2 tablespoons soy sauce
2 tablespoons fresh lemon juice
6 tablespoons extra-virgin olive oil
¼ teaspoon freshly ground black pepper

Whisk together the truffle juice, soy sauce, lemon juice, oil, and pepper until well combined. Whisk again just before using. The dressing can be covered and refrigerated for up to 3 days.

VARIATIONS Proceed as above but with the following ingredients and measurements:

3 tablespoons soy sauce
3 tablespoons fresh lemon juice
5 tablespoons extra-virgin olive oil
1 tablespoon truffle oil

OR

3 tablespoons soy sauce
3 tablespoons fresh lemon juice
5 tablespoons extra-virgin olive oil
1 tablespoon water

garlic aïoli

MAKES ABOUT ½ CUP

HOMEMADE MAYONNAISE is one of life's perfect foods. With a hint of garlic, it's even better. Obviously, this is great on any sandwich, especially a steak or grilled fish sandwich. But it also makes a wonderful dipping sauce. I love it with shellfish, like steamers and grilled lobster. I've lived in this country for a long time now, but I still dunk my French fries in mayonnaise. That's arguably the best use for this simple sauce.

1 small lemon
1 large egg yolk
2 teaspoons Dijon mustard
1 teaspoon finely chopped garlic
½ teaspoon kosher salt
¼ teaspoon freshly ground black pepper
½ cup extra-virgin olive oil

Finely grate the zest of the lemon into a medium bowl. Add the yolk, mustard, garlic, salt, and pepper. Whisk until well blended. Continue whisking while adding the oil in a slow, steady stream to emulsify the mixture. Squeeze 1 tablespoon lemon juice into the mixture and whisk until blended. The aïoli can be covered and refrigerated overnight.

sriracha mayonnaise

MAKES 1 CUP

I'VE DUBBED this my "special sauce." I use it on every single thing—no joke. I've eaten it with savory dishes from artichokes and asparagus to grilled steak and roasted chicken. I've even had it with pineapple and mango. If you have a siphon at home, try it with this. It turns a luscious mayo into an ethereal, creamy foam.

1 large egg yolk
1 tablespoon Dijon mustard
½ teaspoon kosher salt
¾ cup grapeseed or other neutral oil
2 teaspoons fresh lemon juice
2 teaspoons sriracha (see Pantry, page 253)

Whisk together the yolk, mustard, and salt until well blended. Continue whisking while adding the oil in a slow, steady stream to emulsify the mixture. Whisk in the lemon juice and sriracha until well blended. The mayonnaise can be refrigerated for up to 2 days.

russian dressing

MAKES ABOUT 2½ CUPS

WHEN I DECIDED to open my first steakhouse, I knew I needed to have this sauce. Not for a burger, but for a sliced tomato salad. I wanted to riff on the classic by incorporating French cornichons for pickles and Asian ingredients, like miso and sriracha. The result is intensely flavorful. I love this over slow-baked salmon, but also enjoy it on sandwiches. I've even used it in place of mayo in chicken salad and as a dip for crisp, thin onion rings.

10 cornichons (2 ounces)
1 large egg yolk
3 tablespoons white (shiro) miso (see Pantry, page 253)
2½ tablespoons Dijon mustard
2 tablespoons red wine vinegar
⅔ cup grapeseed or other neutral oil
2 tablespoons extra-virgin olive oil
1¼ cups ketchup, preferably organic Heinz
2 teaspoons sriracha (see Pantry, page 253)

Combine the cornichons, yolk, miso, mustard, vinegar, and 1 tablespoon water in a food processor. Pulse until the cornichons are just chopped. With the machine running, add the oils in a steady stream until the mixture is emulsified. Transfer to a large bowl. Stir in the ketchup and sriracha until fully incorporated. The dressing can be covered and refrigerated for up to 3 days.

smoked chile glaze

MAKES 1½ CUPS

ON THE WEEKENDS, barbecue sauce shows up at nearly every meal. I've made countless versions over the years, but this is still one of my favorites. I draw flavors from around the globe to get just the right balance of sweet, spicy, and tangy. You can brush this on any meat while it's grilling to build a sticky glaze. When mixed with homemade mayonnaise, it becomes an amazing spread.

½ cup passion fruit puree (see Pantry, page 253)
1 dried ancho chile, stemmed and roughly chopped
1 dried chipotle chile, stemmed and roughly chopped
¾ cup ketchup, preferably organic Heinz
3 tablespoons red wine vinegar
2 tablespoons unsulphured blackstrap molasses
2 tablespoons garlic powder
2 tablespoons onion powder
1½ tablespoons kecap manis (see Pantry, page 253)
2 teaspoons nam pla
¾ teaspoon liquid mesquite smoke
   (see Pantry, page 253)
½ teaspoon sesame oil
¼ teaspoon kosher salt

Bring the passion fruit puree to a boil over high heat in a small saucepan. Reduce the heat to medium and simmer until the puree is syrupy and reduced by half.

Transfer to a blender and add the chiles, ketchup, vinegar, molasses, garlic and onion powders, kecap manis, nam pla, liquid smoke, sesame oil, and salt. Blend, scraping down the sides of the blender occasionally, until smooth. The sauce can be covered and refrigerated for up to 1 week.

barbecue sauce

MAKES ABOUT ¾ CUP

LESS IS MORE in this simple glaze. The complexity here comes from cooking the garlic and onion until sweet enough to round out the heat of the chiles. I love brushing this on any grilled meat or fish. Another fun use is tossing this sauce with fried calamari or popcorn shrimp.

6 tablespoons extra-virgin olive oil
5 large garlic cloves, minced
½ small sweet onion, finely diced
2 teaspoons kosher salt
2 to 3 chipotle chiles in adobo, chopped, to taste
3 tablespoons plus 1 teaspoon red wine vinegar
2 tablespoons plus 2 teaspoons unsulphured blackstrap molasses
1 tablespoon liquid mesquite smoke
   (see Pantry, page 253)

In a medium sauté pan, heat the oil over medium-low heat. Add the garlic, onion, and salt. Cook, stirring occasionally, until the vegetables are very tender and sweet, about 5 minutes. Stir in the chiles, vinegar, molasses, and liquid smoke until well combined. Transfer the mixture to a blender and puree until almost smooth. The sauce can be covered and refrigerated for up to 3 days.

scotch bonnet hot sauce

MAKES 2 CUPS

THIS IS MORE than just hot sauce. The funky, fruity blend can sear your tongue, but in a pleasant tingling way that allows you to still taste the layers of flavors. You can use this the way you use bottled hot sauce—for buttery sauces, soups, eggs—you'll find that it just makes everything taste so much better.

3 ounces Scotch bonnet chiles (6 to 7), stemmed and seeded (see Note)
1 orange or red bell pepper, stemmed, seeded, and chopped
5 (4-inch) strips fresh orange zest (removed with a vegetable peeler)
½ small garlic clove
2½ tablespoons elderflower cordial (see Pantry, page 252) or sugar
4 teaspoons kosher salt
1 cup champagne vinegar
½ teaspoon guar gum (see Pantry, page 252 or 1 tablespoon cornstarch dissolved in 1 tablespoon water

Combine the chiles, pepper, zest, garlic, 2 tablespoons of the cordial, and 2 teaspoons of the salt in a blender. Pulse until coarsely ground. Transfer to an airtight container and let stand in a warm place for at least 12 hours and up to 1 day to ferment.

Pour the mixture into the blender and add the vinegar, remaining ½ tablespoon cordial, and remaining 2 teaspoons salt. Blend until very smooth. Strain through a medium-mesh sieve, pressing on the solids to extract as much liquid as possible. Discard the solids.

Stir in the guar gum until dissolved. (If using the cornstarch, bring the sauce to a boil and stir in the cornstarch mixture. Cook until thickened, about 1 minute, then let cool to room temperature.) The sauce can be covered and refrigerated for up to 1 week.

note Scotch bonnet peppers are among the hottest in the world—and they make this sauce simply amazing. To tone down the heat, you must remove the seeds. And you must wear rubber or latex gloves while doing it. You'll regret it if you do this bare-handed.

pickled long red chiles

MAKES ABOUT 1 CUP

PICKLING CHILES sounds so much more difficult than it really is. For homemade, all-natural pickled chiles, simply cover them with vinegar. They soften while retaining a little bite and get even hotter while developing a headier flavor. Their acidic pop and bright heat make these my go-to condiment.

2 long red (finger) chiles, sliced crosswise ¼ inch thick
1 cup red wine vinegar or Japanese rice vinegar, plus more as needed

Put the chiles in a nonreactive container. Pour in the vinegar, adding more if needed to cover the chiles. Cover and refrigerate for at least 2 hours or up to 1 week.

yuzu pickles

I LOVE A good bread and butter pickle, so I decided to create my own version. While I don't have the classic spices here, my blend of rice vinegar and yuzu juice approximates the same acidity of the original. These are terrific with (or on) sandwiches. Of course, I like to eat them straight, too.

1 large European cucumber
   (1 pound)
3 fresh green Thai chiles, halved lengthwise
1¾ cups Japanese rice vinegar
¾ cup sugar
2 teaspoons kosher salt
6 tablespoons yuzu juice
   (see Pantry, page 253)

With a vegetable peeler, remove strips of cucumber peel lengthwise ½ inch apart to create vertical stripes. Use a mandoline or very sharp knife to cut the cucumber crosswise into ⅛-inch slices. Transfer to a nonreactive container.

Combine the chiles, vinegar, sugar, and salt in a small saucepan. Bring to a boil, stirring to dissolve the sugar. Remove from the heat and cool to room temperature.

Stir the yuzu juice into the chile mixture and pour over the cucumbers. Cover and refrigerate for at least 4 hours or up to 2 days.

fresh pasta dough

IF YOU'VE ALWAYS wanted to try making your own pasta dough, this is the recipe to start with. I leave the work of kneading to my stand mixer, though I prefer to roll the dough through my hand crank machine. This basic recipe can be turned into any strand pasta and also makes a great ravioli wrapper.

1⅓ cups fine semolina flour
3 large egg yolks
1 large egg
1 teaspoon extra-virgin
   olive oil

Combine the flour, egg yolks, egg, and olive oil in an electric mixer fitted with the dough hook. Mix until the dough comes together, scraping down the bowl as needed. Continue mixing in the machine for 9 minutes to knead the dough well.

Wrap tightly with plastic and let stand at room temperature for 30 minutes before rolling through a pasta machine.

pizza dough MAKES ABOUT 1 POUND, OR ENOUGH FOR 4 INDIVIDUAL PIZZAS

TO MAKE the dough taste like more than just plain bread, I proof it for 8 hours. Once you start working with it, use a light touch. Overworking the dough makes it tough and hard to shape.

3¾ cups all-purpose flour, plus more for shaping
1 teaspoon active dry yeast
1 tablespoon kosher salt
1 tablespoon sugar
Extra-virgin olive oil

Combine the flour, yeast, salt, and sugar in a mixer fitted with the dough hook. Mix until just blended, then add 1⅓ cups warm water. Mix until the dough comes together, then mix for another minute.

Lightly oil a large bowl. Transfer the dough to the bowl, lightly oil the top of the dough, and cover the bowl tightly with plastic wrap. Let rise in a warm spot for 8 hours or until the risen dough is marshmallowy.

On a lightly floured surface, use a bench scraper or sharp knife to divide the dough into quarters. With lightly floured hands, shape the pieces into balls by cupping the dough and turning it against the floured surface until round and tight.

Transfer the balls to a lightly oiled baking sheet or bowls, then lightly brush the tops with oil. Cover loosely with plastic wrap and let rise in a warm spot until tripled in volume, about 1½ hours. Use immediately or put a sheet of parchment on top of the dough balls, then cover tightly with plastic wrap. Refrigerate for up to 2 days. When ready to use, remove from the refrigerator and let stand in a warm place for 1 hour.

pâte brisée MAKES ENOUGH FOR TWO 8-INCH TARTS

MY GRANDMOTHER taught me how to make this basic pastry when I was young. The one thing I learned simply by eating her endless variations on delicious tarts for dinner every night is that this dough can be used for just about anything—sweet or savory.

1¾ cups all-purpose flour, plus more as needed
½ teaspoon kosher salt
6 tablespoons (¾ stick) unsalted butter, preferably cultured, cut up and chilled
2 tablespoons plus 1 teaspoon vegetable shortening, chilled
1 large egg

In a mixer fitted with the paddle attachment, mix the flour, salt, butter, and shortening on low speed until crumbly. With the machine running, add 2 tablespoons cold water and the egg. Beat just until the dough comes together in large clumps.

Divide the dough in half and press each half into a 1-inch-thick round disk. Wrap each tightly in plastic and refrigerate until firm, at least 1 hour or up to 3 days; let stand at room temperature for 15 minutes before rolling. Alternatively, the dough can be frozen for up to 1 month; thaw in the refrigerator overnight.

For each crust, on a lightly floured surface with a lightly floured rolling pin, roll 1 piece of dough into a 10-inch round. Carefully transfer the dough to an 8-inch round fluted tart pan with a removable bottom, pressing the dough gently against the bottom and up the sides. If necessary, trim the edges against the rim.

Line the dough with foil, then fill with dried beans or pie weights. Freeze overnight, or until very hard.

To blind bake a tart shell, preheat the oven to 375°F.

Bake the frozen crust until the edges are set, about 20 minutes. Remove the foil and beans. Poke holes all over the bottom of the crust with a fork, then return to the oven. Bake until the bottom is set and the crust is blonde, about 8 minutes. Let cool in the pan on a rack.

caramel sauce

MAKES ABOUT 1½ CUPS

THE TRIO OF sugar, cream, and butter can't be beat. In its liquid form here, it can be drizzled on desserts—or even breakfast treats.

1 cup sugar
⅓ cup heavy cream, at room temperature
5 tablespoons unsalted butter, preferably cultured, at
    room temperature

Put the sugar in a large saucepan. Add just enough water to dampen it. Cook over medium-high heat, stirring, until the sugar dissolves. Continue cooking until amber, swirling the pan occasionally.

Remove from the heat and stir in the cream—be careful, the mixture will bubble up—and then the butter. Continue stirring until the mixture is well blended. Let cool to room temperature. The sauce can be covered and refrigerated for up to 2 days.

crème anglaise

MAKES ABOUT 1¼ CUPS

INSTEAD OF USING cream or half-and-half in this classic dessert sauce, I prefer using milk. It keeps the sauce light, tasty, and simple, but the mixture will not appear as thick as some other versions of crème anglaise. This can be served with any dessert, but I especially like it over fresh fruit.

1 cup whole milk
½ vanilla bean, split lengthwise and seeds scraped
3 large egg yolks
⅓ cup sugar

Whisk together the milk and vanilla seeds and pod in a medium saucepan. Heat over medium-high heat until bubbles just begin to form around the edges.

Meanwhile, rapidly whisk together the yolks and sugar in a medium bowl until the sugar dissolves and the mixture becomes pale yellow.

Continue whisking rapidly and add a few spoonfuls of the just-boiling milk mixture to temper the yolks. Remove the milk mixture from the heat and whisk in the yolk mixture in a steady stream. Set the saucepan over medium-low heat and whisk rapidly until thick enough to coat the back of a spoon, about 7 minutes. When you run your finger across a spoon dipped into the sauce, it should leave a clear line.

Strain through a fine-mesh sieve into a small bowl. Set the bowl on top of a larger bowl of ice and water to stop the mixture from cooking. Let cool to room temperature, stirring occasionally. The sauce can be covered and refrigerated for up to 2 days.

pantry

At home, I cook with easy-to-find pantry staples. (Although I always try to buy the best!) But every once in a while, I like to use ingredients that are well worth searching for—online or in stores. Over the course of my career, I've been thrilled to find that pantry items I once had to track down in specialty shops are now readily available in supermarkets. That may not be true yet for all of the items here, but it probably won't be long before it is.

BONITO FLAKES If you've ever had miso soup, you've tasted the smoky sea flavor of this Japanese staple. These feather-light flakes—made from a dried fish similar to tuna—form the base of dashi, a simple but complex soup stock. I use them all the time, so I keep a big bag at home. But because the flakes go rancid quickly, you should buy smaller packets if you plan to use them only occasionally.

ELDERFLOWER CORDIAL Any Anglophile can tell you that this simple syrup infused with delicate wildflowers makes delicious drinks. I can tell you that it transforms savory sauces, too. BottleGreen is my brand of choice and worth finding online.

FRESH RICOTTA CHEESE Unlike the chalky, tasteless stuff in supermarket cases, fresh ricotta is creamy and slightly sweet. I get mine from Di Palo's in New York City, but you can make your own if you don't live near an Italian market or cheese shop. Simmer 4 cups milk and 1 teaspoon salt, then stir in 3 tablespoons lemon juice. Continue simmering until large curds form. Strain through a cheesecloth-lined fine-mesh sieve for 1 minute, then transfer to an airtight container. Refrigerate until cold.

GUAR GUM Sometimes I want to thicken my sauces without reducing them or adding fat. This powder, extracted from guar beans, does the trick. You need only a little to instantly add viscosity. It even dissolves in cold liquid, making it an extremely versatile ingredient.

KECAP MANIS An Indonesian specialty, this soy sauce sweetened with palm sugar is as thick as molasses. It adds a rich salty-sweetness and syrupy texture to sauces.

KONBU Umami, that intensely savory fifth taste sensation, can easily be achieved with just a little konbu. With a subtle sea-sweetness, this dried kelp is naturally rich in glutamates and heightens the flavors of everything it touches.

LIQUID MESQUITE SMOKE Since I don't always have time to use the smoker in my yard, I use this to add a hint of mesquite to my sauces. Be sure to look for an all-natural, organic version.

MUSTARD OIL I don't know why, but most of the mustard oil sold in the United States is used for massages, hair conditioning, or skin care. Don't buy that stuff. Look for edible mustard oil, found in Indian groceries and used extensively in Indian cooking. When used judiciously, it adds a hit of rounded, mellow heat.

PASSION FRUIT PUREE Not to be confused with passion fruit juice, this is a concentrated puree of just the fruit. With a potent tropical sweet-tartness, it works as well in sauces as in drinks.

SMOKED HOT PAPRIKA Also known as Pimentón de la Vera Picante, this Spanish specialty is made by slowly drying the hot peppers over a wood-burning fire, resulting in a fantastic rich heat. Unless you plan on using it frequently, buy only a small jar. You definitely want this spice to taste fresh.

SRIRACHA I was an early adopter of Huy Fong Foods Sriracha and remain loyal to this all-purpose hot sauce. In its now-iconic green-topped squeeze bottle, it delivers a great zing of heat.

TRUFFLE JUICE Unlike potent truffle oil, this product captures the pure, heady aroma of fresh truffles. Made from the natural juices released when truffles are prepared for preservation, it delivers an intense, clean truffle flavor. It's pricey but well worth it if you're a truffle lover like me.

WHITE (SHIRO) MISO Sometimes also called *saikyo miso*, this is the lightest in color and least salty among miso pastes, which are made from fermented soy beans. Most commonly associated with its eponymous soup, miso is used extensively in Japanese cooking and adds a depth of salty sweetness. In an airtight container, miso will keep for months in the fridge.

YUZU JUICE Squeezed from an extremely tart citrus fruit, this juice delivers an intense, clean citrus flavor. Japanese cooks also use the fruit itself, which isn't available here. The juice, however, can be found in Asian markets. Its potency diminishes with time, so get a smaller bottle and use it quickly.

acknowledgments

At my restaurants, I cook for my customers. They inspire me to create original dishes and to always keep innovating. I'm grateful for the support of diners all over the world.

At home, I cook for my family. They inspire me to make the delicious and deeply personal dishes in this book. Thank you to my wife, Marja, for her unwavering love and support and to our wonderful daughter, Chloe. Thanks to my son, Cedric; my daughter Louise; my daughter-in-law, Ochi; and my grandson, Olivier, for bringing me so much joy. Thanks to my brother Philippe, who's been with me from the start; his wife, Jenny; and their children, Etienne, Alyssa, and Emma.

Thank you to my writer, Genevieve Ko, for her talent, hard work, and friendship, and for turning my recipes and stories into this book.

Thank you to my restaurant family: a special thanks to Greg Brainin and Mark Lapico for lending their time and creativity to this project; to Dan Kluger at ABC; Bernie Sun, my beverage director; and Tamara Wood, my assistant. Thanks to my other chefs and front-of-house staff in all of my restaurants for upholding my standards with hard work and loyalty. Thanks also go to Dan Del Vecchio and to my business partner Phil Suarez and his wife, Lucy.

Thank you to photographer John Kernick, photo art director Erika Oliveira, and stylist Susie Theodorou for combining their talents to create beautiful photographs that capture my food and life at home. Thanks to their assistants: Craig Allen, Vivian Lui, Darrell Taunt, and Rizwan Alvi. Thanks to my friend Magnus Hansson. Thanks to Cynthia Brennan of Table Local Market and to the many other farmers who've grown and raised the ingredients I prepare at home. A very special thanks to Paulette Cole and Amy Chender at ABC Carpet & Home for the gorgeous Zani & Zani cookware and to Stan Barrett and Elisa Waysenson from Lacanche for Art Culinaire for the stunning Lacanche range.

Thank you to the Clarkson Potter team, especially Rica Allannic, Marysarah Quinn, Stephanie Huntwork, Ada Yonenaka, Joan Denman, Ashley Phillips, Doris Cooper, and Lauren Shakely. Thanks to my agent, Angela Miller.

This book is the culmination of a lifetime of eating and cooking. I'm grateful to my parents, Jeanine and Georges, from whom I get my name and my love of food. And I'm thankful for my grandmothers, Berthe Heitz and Mathilde Vongerichten, my first teachers in the kitchen.

—JEAN-GEORGES VONGERICHTEN

Thanks go first and foremost to Jean-Georges, a most brilliant and gracious chef and friend. Thank you to Marja, Chloe, Cedric, Louise, and Philippe for opening your home and sharing your stories. Thanks to Greg, Mark, Dan, Bernie, Tamara, and the whole Jean-Georges team for all your contributions to this project. Thanks to John, Erika, Susie, Craig, Vivian, Darrell, Rizwan, Magnus, Rica, Marysarah, Stephanie, Ashley, and Angela for a beautiful book. Thanks to the many friends and colleagues who've been a source of encouragement over the years. Finally, thanks to my family, especially my husband, David, and my daughters, Natalie, Vivien, and Charlotte, for your patience and love.

—GENEVIEVE KO

index